The

Grits®
Girls Raised In The South

Guide
to Life

The

Grits.

Girls Raised In The South

Guide
to Life

Deborah Ford
with Edie Hand

DUTTON

DUTTON
Published by Penguin Group (USA) Inc. 375 Hudson Street, New York, New York 10014, U.S.A.
Penguin Books Ltd, Registered Offices: 80 Strand, London WC2R 0RL, England
Penguin Books Australia Ltd, 250 Camberwell Road, Camberwell, Victoria 3124, Australia
Penguin Books Canada Ltd, 10 Alcorn Avenue, Toronto, Ontario, Canada M4V 3B2
Penguin Books (N.Z.) Ltd, Cnr Rosedale and Airborne Roads, Albany, Auckland 1310, New Zealand

Published by Dutton, a member of Penguin Group (USA) Inc.

First printing, April 2003
10 9 8 7 6 5 4 3 2 1

 REGISTERED TRADEMARK—MARCA REGISTRADA

LIBRARY OF CONGRESS CATALOGING-IN-PUBLICATION DATA
Ford, Deborah.
The Grits (girls raised in the South) guide to life / by Deborarh Ford with Edie Hand.
   p. cm.
ISBN 0-525-94726-4 (alk. paper)
1. Women—Southern States—Social life and customs—Humor. 2. Southern States—Social life and customs—1865—Humor. I. Hand, Edie, 1951— II. Title.
PN6231.S64 F67 2003
818′.5407—dc21   2002192525

Printed in the United States of America
Set in OPTI Worcester Round
Designed by Sabrina Bowers

PUBLISHER'S NOTE
This book is a work of fiction. Names, characters, places, and incidents are either the product of the author's imagination or are used fictitiously, and any resemblance to actual persons, living or dead, business establishments, events, or locales is entirely coincidental.

*T*his book is dedicated to my daughters, Callie and Chesley Michael; their grandmothers, Elizabeth Rogers Fleming and Sybil Hendricks Michael; my sisters, Virginia, Barbara, Rita, and Mavis; my brother Stanley; all of my friends in the "neighborhood"; and to the memory of Edie's brothers, David and Phillip Blackburn, and to the courage of her brother, Terry.

And of course, I dedicate the book especially to all Girls Raised in the South, who I am grateful to count as my true-blue sisters.

—Deborah Ford

Contents

Acknowledgments

I'd like to thank the many people who were instrumental in the completion of this book: my agent, Bret Witter; my editor, Kelly Notaras; and my friends Paula Bennett Paddock, Sandy Eichelberger, Julie Dana, Brandy Clough, Dana Gache, Travis Saucer, Darlene Real, Kathy Hope, Mark Aldridge, Linc Hand, Mitzi Breeze, Kim Pass, Sue Blackburn Hardesty, and Dr. Cathy Davis.

Finally, this book would not have been possible without the support and encouragement of my partner, Don Sallee.

—Deborah Ford

grits \'grits\ *n* :

1 : acronym for Girls Raised In The South
2 : an increasingly popular expression associated with the enviable attributes of Southern women, e.g., absolutely irresistible charm, a relaxed Southern drawl that leaves men hanging on every word, and the natural inclination to be cunning and caring
3 : also refers to a Southern breakfast dish made from ground hominy

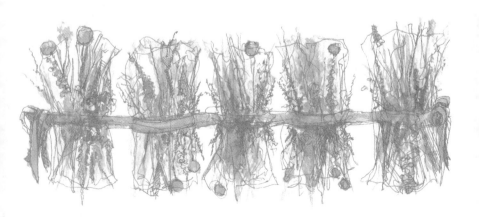

Foreword

As a true blue Southern girl I have often wondered...if preppies could have their own handbook...why not us? And now at last, my two good friends Deborah Ford and Edie Hand have written the definitive handbook for Southern gals raised in the South. One must simply not leave home without it! It deserves a place on your shelf between *Gone With the Wind* and the Memphis Junior League cookbook, and I predict in years to come it will be passed down to daughters along with the family silver and great-grandmother's lace doilies. It is funny, wise, charming, and smart, just like the two gals who wrote it.

As modern Southern women we have learned to network with one another and share all the good advice and recipes and rules of accepted behavior that have been handed down to us (it's a rough world out there). And so in keeping with that wonderful tradition I would like to share some advice my own wise Southern mother gave to me. When I was in high school contemplating whether to take Home Economics or not, my mother exclaimed: "Oh no, darling...you must never learn to cook and clean or they will expect you to do it!" It is advice that has served me well throughout the years. Good luck in all you do!

—Fannie Flagg

Fannie Flagg's
Fried Green Tomatoes

from the Original Whistlestop Cafe

To keep the cooked tomatoes from getting soggy before they are served, stand them up like wheels in the serving dish instead of stacking them.

¾ cup self-rising flour
¼ cup cornmeal
¼ teaspoon salt
¼ teaspoon pepper
¾ cup milk
3 to 4 green tomatoes, cut into ¼-inch slices
Vegetable oil

Combine first 5 ingredients; mix until smooth. Add additional milk to thin, if necessary; batter should resemble pancake batter. Working in batches, dip tomato slices into batter, allowing excess batter to drip back into bowl. Fry in 2 inches hot oil (375°) in a large heavy skillet until browned, turning once carefully with tongs. Transfer to a colander to drain.

Yield: 3 to 4 servings

Introduction

*"What can be more Southern than to
obsess about being Southern?"*
—Elizabeth Fortson Arroyo

What makes a Girl Raised in the South so very extraordinary? Why, it's the very essence of who we are—our style, our heritage, and our upbringing. We're remarkably distinct and hopelessly in love with our history and tradition. Known far and wide for our femininity, charm, hospitality, and beauty, we're mighty proud of what we say to the world.

It's often said that we Southerners get our charm from our historically aristocratic background, and that's partly true—what is known today as "Southern culture" began three centuries ago with the European settlers who came to our region. But real Southern character isn't about mansions and plantations—it's about ordinary people, of all races and backgrounds, who go the extra mile to live life with dignity, style, class, and pride even in today's fast and furious world. What does this mean for you, dear reader? It means that absolutely anyone can learn the secrets of Southern charm, no matter where you're from or who your people are.

How, you ask? Well honey, that's what *we're* here for!

What you hold in your hands is a down-home, bona fide Southern primer. Seeing as how we Southern women are committed to the practice of hospitality (see Part III, *Southern Hospitality*), we'd never leave you to figure out the ingredients for mixing up that special Grits charm all by yourself. No indeed! In fact, we've cooked up a whole section dedicated to *The Basic Ingredients* (Part I) that make a Southern girl unique. And for those of you who may be slower to catch on than most, bless your hearts, we've chosen an utterly Southern symbol to represent each one of these very important traits:

The **Magnolia Tree** for strength of character
The **Iron Skillet** for Southern flavor
The **String of Pearls** for beauty, both natural and cultured

Southern girls know their grits:

- Cheese
- Garlic
- Stone-ground

Once we're all clear on what Grits are made of, it'll be time to teach you a little about acting like one! We'll show you how to talk like a Girl Raised in the South (Chapter 4, "Saying Darlin' Like You Mean It"), how to eat like one (Chapter 6, "I Do Believe You Ate My Salad"), how to entertain like one (Chapter 10, "Putting on the Grits"). We'll explain the intricacies of the Southern wedding (Chapter 11, "Let Them Eat Cake"), help you untangle your family tree—Southern style (Chapter

17, "The Ties That Bind [And Sometimes Strangle]"), and give you a tour through our Grits "Hall of Fame" (Chapter 18, "Making Us Proud"). And that's just the tip of the iceberg: there's also Southern humor (Chapter 12), Southern sports (Chapter 15), and—Praise the Lawd!—even Southern religion (Chapter 14).

Above all else, this book is full to brimming with Southern pride. We hope that after reading *The Grits Guide to Life* you, too, will want to be a Grits girl. Whether you were born and bred below the Mason-Dixon line, or just want to have that Southern polish (Grits also stands for Girls *Refined* in the South, after all!), this book has everything you need to be the beautiful belle you've always wanted to be. Learn our history, follow our "do's" and "don'ts," and practice your wit, charm, and style daily. Before long you'll find you've become a genuine smooth-talking, card-toting, sweet-as-sugar Southern belle to make Miss Scarlett *proud!*

So pull up a chair. Sit for a spell. The book you hold in your hands will teach you everything you need to know about life, Southern girl style.

—Deborah Ford *with* Edie Hand

GRITS PEARL OF WISDOM #1:

Grits are eaten with butter, gravy, or cheese—never sugar

Cheesy Grits Casserole

1 cup grits (quick or regular)
½ cup margarine
3 eggs, beaten
⅔ cup sweet milk
½ pound cheddar cheese
½ pound fried bacon, crumbled (optional)

Cook grits according to package instructions. Add margarine to hot grits and stir until melted. Add cheese and stir. Combine eggs with milk and stir into grits. Add crumbled bacon. Pour into greased 2-quart casserole dish. Sprinkle extra cheese on top if you desire. Bake 30 to 40 minutes at 325 until mixture is set and lightly browned. (The center is the last to cook.)

Yield: 8 to 12 servings

PART I

The Basic Ingredients

CHAPTER 1

Grits Are Magnolias:

Our Strength of Character

"It is a special vanity of Southern women to believe that they are different from other American women."
—Sharon McKern, author of *Redneck Mothers,
Good Ol' Girls and Other Southern Belles*

$\mathcal{A}$NYONE WHO'S SPENT TIME BELOW THE Mason-Dixon line knows this truth: Southern women are anything but ordinary. Our unique, often unspoken code of conduct has allowed us to survive good times and bad, and never lose the sense of who we are. Margaret Mitchell, the belle of Southern female writers, got it right when she had Scarlett O'Hara come down the stairs in a dress made out of curtains: a Southern girl knows that pride and endurance always come before vanity. Our character is both created by, and essential to, the fabric of our society. Without the strength of the Southern girl, the South couldn't have

"The biggest myth about Southern women is that we are frail types—fainting on our sofas . . . nobody where I grew up ever acted like that. We were about as fragile as coal trucks."

—*Lee Smith, North Carolina Grits and author of* The Last Girls

survived its rich and rocky history; without history, on the other hand, the Southern girl wouldn't be who she is today.

It's sometimes suggested (by Yankees, we'd wager) that Grits are one-dimensional. This is not surprising: those who don't understand us see only our outward devotion to femininity and charm. What they are missing is the fact that, like the magnolia tree, our beautiful blossoms are the outward expression of the strength that lies beneath.

GRITS PEARL OF WISDOM #2:

Learn from the magnolia and don't let grass grow beneath your feet. Keep moving, and live life to the fullest.

Like the Grits girl, the majestic magnolia tree is indigenous to the South, having spread its deep roots in our rich soil for centuries. The magnolia is a wide and solid tree, with large waxy

GRITS GLOSSARY

steel magnolia \ stē(ə)l mag-'nōl-yə \ *n* : *a Southern woman who has weathered tragedy and heartache while retaining pride, dignity, and a love of life; often used to describe an older woman who has taken it upon herself to teach the younger generation the Southern way of life; one of the highest honors a Grits can achieve. Ex.: Scarlett O'Hara*

leaves that provide so much shade even the hardiest Southern grass has trouble thriving beneath its limbs. But despite its grand strength and powerful presence, the magnolia tree produces some of the most delicate, fragrant white flowers around.

Magnolia trees are simply *made* for a front yard—right alongside that other Southern staple, the dogwood tree. Not only do they provide beautiful flowers in May and June, they provide shade, privacy, and an intoxicating scent. Magnolias will grow almost anywhere in the United States, although in the North they will usually only reach ten to twenty feet in height—proving once again that everything is bigger and better in the South!

The Southern Magnolia tree...

... is the state tree of Mississippi
... produces the state flower of both Mississippi and Louisiana
... grows throughout the South in rich, moist soil
... is indigenous to warm, temperate, and semitropical climates
... can be cut for lumber
... may grow sixty to eighty feet tall

Your Very Own Magnolia Tree

*H*ere are some simple instructions on planting and caring for a magnolia tree. Planting a magnolia—no matter where you reside—is a great way to begin your transformation into a true Grits:

1. Magnolias should be planted as saplings, when they are three to six feet in height. Plant them with the burlap-covered root ball intact.

2. Magnolias need rich soil and can grow anywhere from full sunlight to partial shade. Because of their full branches, plant the tree at least ten feet from a house or other structure.

3. Plant magnolias in fall or late winter. That will give them plenty of time to adapt before the dry summer months.

4. Water a young magnolia very heavily several times a week. After the first year, the magnolia should survive on its own, except in times of drought.

5. Magnolia flowers can be clipped for decoration, but they dry quickly and don't have long stems like other flowers. They are best floated in a shallow bowl of water with two or three other blossoms.

continues...

6. Never trim a magnolia! You will ruin its beautiful shape. If you must trim the tree, hire a professional who has worked with magnolias before.

7. Don't bother planting grass under a magnolia. It's a lost cause, sugah!

Like Grits, magnolias stand as a symbol of all that is good about the South. If we Grits are nurtured when we're young, we'll grow up to be self-sustaining and strong. We blossom into beautiful adulthood because we have our roots firmly planted in our native soil, nurtured by family traditions and history. And, like magnolia trees, we're found all over the country—wherever the conditions are right. Both magnolias and Grits symbolize beauty, perseverance, strength, and patience.

GRITS PEARL OF WISDOM #3:

Men must understand that, like a magnolia, you can't trim a Grits: we are perfect just as we are.

CHAPTER 2

Grits Are Iron Skillets:

The Flavoring of the South

"Can't no Teflon fry no fried chicken."
—Vertamae Grosvenor, *Vibration Cooking,*
or The Travel Notes of a Geechee Girl

WOMEN ARE WOMEN, SOME PEOPLE SAY, regardless of where they are born. Please! Haven't they ever heard the saying "you are what you eat"? The Southern flavor is bred in us from the moment we enter this world and have our first meal. Our food nurtures and sustains us, all the while imbuing us with the unique Southern style that we will carry throughout the course of our lives.

Indeed, the center of the Southern family has always been the kitchen. Traditionally, it's the place where all the work inside the house gets done, where a family can crowd around a fire on a cold winter night with the smell of fried chicken or biscuits still hovering in the air. The kitchen is a place where families slow down, pull up a chair, and talk to one another. This is part of the reason our cuisine is known the world over as "comfort food."

GRITS GLOSSARY

iron skillet \'ī(-ə)rn 'ski-lət\ *n* : *a frying pan cast out of a lustrous, malleable, and durable metal alloy, suitable for cooking a variety of Southern foods including fried chicken, slow-cooked greens, and biscuits; a treasured heirloom.*

At the same time, Grits know the kitchen is more about attitude than appetite. In this modern world, there is no reason for a woman to have to slave over a hot stove: so don't feel obligated! Cooking a great meal isn't one of the requirements of being a Grits; it's a bonus that others should appreciate, not expect.

Even if she doesn't cook much, there is no more important heirloom to a true Grits than Mama's iron skillet. The iron skillet is *the* essential tool of Southern country cooking, and as such it is a prized possession that is passed down from generation to generation, gathering unique character along the way. While most modern cookware is cheaply constructed and easily damaged, an iron skillet can be passed on for years. It's a tangible symbol of the tradition and heritage that are the cornerstones of the Grits lifestyle.

Like the Southern girl, the skillet is durable and trustworthy, and imparts its own flavor to whatever it touches. It's this one-of-a-kind quality that has caused many an unfortunate incident between Southern daughters when the time has

LARGE SKILLET
- Fried Chicken
- Fried Okra
- Cornbread

Alice Hood-Hacker's
Buttermilk Biscuits

Alice Hood-Hacker, Mississippi Grits, raised twelve children, fifty-five grandchildren, and eighteen great-grandchildren on this tried-and-true recipe. She even had a famous relative who would sometimes drop by for a bite—a Mississippi boy named Elvis Presley.

Biscuits:
2 cups self-rising flour
1½ teaspoons baking powder
¼ teaspoon baking soda
1 teaspoon sugar
½ cup shortening
1 cup buttermilk

Preheat oven to 450°. In a large bowl, combine the flour, baking powder, soda, and sugar. Cut in the shortening with a pastry blender or two knives. Add the buttermilk and knead until smooth and pliable. Roll the dough out on a floured surface to the desired thickness, or about a ½ inch. Cut with a biscuit cutter and place in a flat iron skillet. Bake for about 12 minutes or until brown on top.

Yield: 10 servings

Chocolate Gravy

2 tablespoons cocoa
1½ cups sugar
2 tablespoons all-purpose flour
1 teaspoon vanilla extract
3 cups water

In a saucepan, combine the cocoa, sugar, flour, vanilla, and water, and cook over medium heat until it boils. The mixture will slowly thicken. Cook for about 10 minutes. Pour over buttered hot biscuits.

come for Mama to pass the skillet on to the next generation. Our lives may not revolve around the kitchen anymore, but every Grits girl knows the way to a man's heart is through his stomach!

"Seasoning" is the process of applying layers of natural oils to a new skillet in order to create a nonstick surface. Enhanced over time by repeated use, the seasoning not only keeps food from adhering to the inside of the pan but it also imparts a rich, unique flavor to whatever food is cooked in the skillet. This is why regular cookware can't compare—the *flavor* just isn't there! Keep in mind that when you purchase an iron skillet it will be medium gray in color, but will start turning darker with seasoning. The pitch-black color of a well-used skillet is something of which a Southern girl can be very proud.

WELL, I DECLARE!:

True cast-iron skillets are molded, so each has a "scar" on its side or bottom where the molten iron was poured into the mold. That's not a blemish, girls, it's a mark of authenticity!

Seasoning Your Iron Skillet

1. Heat the oven to 250°–300°.

2. Coat the pan with lard or bacon grease. Do not use liquid vegetable oil because it will leave a sticky surface that will interfere with the seasoning process.

3. Put the pan in the oven. In 15 minutes, remove the pan and pour out any excess grease. Place the pan back in the oven and bake for 2 hours.

Repeating this process several times will help create a stronger seasoning bond. Also, when you put the pan into service, it is recommended to use it initially for foods high in fat—bacon is a good choice—because the grease from these foods will help strengthen the seasoning.

Skillet Season

BY SANDY EICHELBERGER, ALABAMA GRITS

I heard the sound of clanking metal and I knew Arbner had arrived. Each morning when she came to care for the babies and tidy the house, she stopped at the kitchen stove to begin the ritual of seasoning my new iron skillet. This had gone on for well over a month and I had begun to regret ever buying the darn thing. The sound of clanking metal and slamming cabinet doors before eight o'clock every morning was almost unbearable. She would heat the oven, give the skillet a good "greasin'," and plop it in the oven for its daily "seasonin' session." She only removed it as she left in the afternoon.

The skillet was not a pleasant subject between Arbner and me. I was in my mid-twenties and she had to be over seventy, so according to her I still needed "tendin.'" She always had a lecture waiting for me on baby-rearing, cooking, or just life in general. I would hear her mumbling low, "I don't know why she went out of here and bought a bran'-new fryin' pan—she oughta known better than that." I would smile to myself and hope that would be the only admonishment I would receive that day.

One morning, I listened to the banging and mumbling in the distance as I looked down at my beautiful baby girl. As I gazed at her little porcelain face, I realized I held in my lap an unseasoned skillet. Every day I would slowly and patiently "season" her in hopes that she would one day become the lovely Southern lady we all want our daughters to be. It is a slow and tedious process. Southern belles and Southern skillets—don't get in a hurry on either one. It's an hour-by-hour, day-by-day, lifetime endeavor.

SMALL SKILLET

- Sauces and Cornbread

MEDIUM SKILLET

- Fried Green Tomatoes
- Cream Corn
- Fried Squash
- Cornbread and Biscuits
- Gravy

The Skillet Wars

My sister Mavis and I used to argue all the time over who would get Grandma Emma's skillet. Throughout high school our favorite game was to hide the skillet from one another, since we both wanted the pan that held such fond memories of Grandma's mouthwatering cornbread. When Mother passed away last year I searched the kitchen for that skillet, but I have yet to find it. I know she didn't take it with her—for heaven's sake, what would the neighbors think!? Probably a good thing I haven't called my sister in a while, because if I find out she's got that skillet I really don't know what I'll call her!

—Deborah Ford

Just as modern nonstick cookware requires special cleaning techniques, your iron skillet needs its own brand of tender loving care.

- Clean the cookware while it is still hot by rinsing with warm water and scraping away any leftover food. Do not use a scouring pad or soap; they will break down the pan's seasoning. And never, ever put your iron skillet in the dishwasher!

- Do not store food in the cast-iron skillet. The acids present in most foods will break down the seasoning, while the iron will cause your leftovers to take on a metallic flavor.

- Store your iron skillet without the lid, especially in humid weather, to avoid a buildup of moisture that can cause rust. Should rust appear, the iron skillet must be reseasoned.

GRITS PEARL OF WISDOM #4:

Never, ever let someone else clean your skillet—strangers are not to be trusted with this valuable gem!

The iron skillet is a symbol of Southern heritage in that it represents the importance of our ancestors and their customs, innovations, and accomplishments. A Southern girl who values her heirloom skillet will also understand the value of her manners, her appearance, and her family name. In the South, the iron skillet is simply a part of who we are.

Just like Southern girls, though, no two iron skillets are the same. Each bears the marks of its heritage in the form of scratches, scrapes, and dents, and each has its own special use. Get to know your skillet and treat it well, and you can look forward to a lifetime of compliments on your cooking—from your light-as-a-feather biscuits to your finger-licking chicken.

Not that a Southern woman would evah lick her fingers . . . in public, anyway!

CHAPTER 3

Grits Are Pearls:

Southern Beauty, Natural and Cultured

"One never has to justify buying a strand of pearls."
—common knowledge among Southern women

No ONE CAN ARGUE WITH THE FACT THAT Southern girls are some of the most beautiful our nation has to offer, thanks both to our well-bred stock and our scrupulous attention to the details of beauty. It's this beauty, natural and—*ahem*—"cultured," that makes a Southern girl just like a string of pearls.

Style, grace, and elegance are a Southern girl's greatest assets, worn as proudly as a young girl's first strand of pearls. Like the Southern girl, these pearls are tough, resilient, and smooth, and represent the purest of nature's gifts.

GRITS GLOSSARY

natural pearls \\'na-chə-r l 'per(-ə)ls\\ *n* : *rare and very expensive pearls found in nature, mostly in the oyster beds of the South Pacific, and worn by Southern women of high pedigree and even higher standards who—for Daddy and their men, anyway—are themselves very expensive*

Few people realize that pearls are also indigenous to the South. In colonial times, pearls were found naturally off the Southern coast—and even in the Mississippi and Tennessee

Rivers! Ever since these early days pearls have been treasured for their beauty, and have been a sign of prestige among wealthy Southern families.

cultured pearls \ 'kəl-chəred 'pər(-ə)ls\ *n*: *pearls created by man, through the insertion of an irritant—usually a grain of sand—inside the shell of an oyster; worn by similarly cultured Southern belles ranging in circumstance from the country club to the trailer park*

When cultured pearls were first produced in the early 1900s, pearl fever caught on with the common folk as well. They are just as beautiful as natural pearls, because they are cultivated naturally, after receiving a helping hand from man.

Pearl Pop Quiz

See if you can tell the real from the faux: match the strings on the left with theri trype on the right! (See Below for answers).

A. 1. Real

B. 2. Cultured

C. 3. Faux

Answers: Honey, if you can't tell, why should we?

faux pearls \ 'fō 'pər(-ə)ls\ *n* : *A combination of paste and putty, these pearls are simply good copies of the real thing.*

Since they were cheaper than natural pearls, they gave even ordinary women the opportunity to dress like royalty. And as every Grits girl knows, looking good at half the price is what sets you apart in the gossip circle. Most importantly, cultured pearls prove what Southern girls have always known—that you don't have to be born to the aristocracy to be treated like a queen!

The Pearl Girls

A group of my girlfriends—mostly teachers I worked with—was enjoying one of our "hen parties" when the discussion turned to the Ya Yas and the Sweet Potato Queens. We think they are just darlin' girls, but we decided there was room for a different sort of group—one that *any* girl could enjoy! "Well, pearls are universal," said my friend Jennifer. "We can be the Pearl Girls." We all loved the idea, and a new Southern sisterhood was born!

—Deborah Ford

Applications available upon request for anyone with a string of pearls.

Taking Care of Your Pearls

- Carefully store your pearls in a special pouch or jewelry box to keep them safe from scratches.
- Keep your pearls far away from hairspray, cosmetics, and perfumes.
- Necklaces should be removed while playing sports. (However, you may keep those pearl earrings in.)

Cultured pearls have something else to teach us about Girls Raised in the South: Grits aren't born, they're *made*. The essential characteristics of integrity, toughness, elegance, and style are built up over the years through social, family, and religious traditions.

A note for those unfortunate enough to have been born somewhere other than the American South: just as a string of

A Grits girl treated without TLC may end up a PMS . . . a Precious Moody Southerner!

faux pearls, worn right, can invoke the same beauty as the real thing, so too can you become a part of the Grits club! All you need is a dash of Dixie, a pinch of attitude, and a cupful of that

Elvis's Grandmother's Pearls

The Presley family didn't have much (not until Elvis got famous, anyway) but they did have pearls. My grandmother Alice and great-aunt Minnie—Elvis Presley's grandmother—each had a double strand of pearls that had been given to them by their mother, my great-grandmother Ader Hood. Even though they were faux, they were prominently displayed in each home, draped over the "book of pearls"—the Bible.

The pearls were worn, too, but only on special occasions—church, funerals, and weddings. Later Elvis gave grandmother Minnie a strand of *real* pearls, which was eventually passed down to me. I treasure this gift from Elvis, and keep the pearls draped over the family Bible in my home today. I look forward to passing them on to the next generation, as a symbol of our heritage.

—Edie Hand

special kind of beauty that only gets better with time: the inner kind.

Real or faux, a strand of pearls is a mark of gentility that can be worn for any occasion—from the tennis court to the cocktail hour to the summer wedding. We may keep them safe in our jewelry boxes or on the family Bible as a reminder of what we hold dear; we may wear them every day or just on Sundays. But pearls, like Southern girls, must be handled with care.

As with the iron skillet, pearls are lovingly passed down

from generation to generation, from mother to daughter, aunt to aunt, friend to friend or—in some cases—from ex-mother-in-law to ex-daughter-in-law. If iron skillets are the practical side of our heritage, pearls are our flamboyant beauty and style.

WELL, I DECLARE!:
Cultured pearls were invented in 1906 by Kokichi Mikimoto, the son of a noodle-maker in Japan, when he patented a way to induce oysters to make perfectly round pearls on demand. His company, Mikimoto, is still famous around the world for its quality pearls.

It's the pride that comes with knowing you come from a long line of strong, independent, and beautifully appointed Southern Belles—even if your family tree is a little crooked in spots.

PART II

Southern Style

CHAPTER 4

Saying Darlin'
Like You Mean It:

The Grits Guide to Speech

"The drawl—which accents the rhapsodic blend of beauty, grace, charm, ingenuity, and strength—is the gorgeous red bow that completes the [Grits] package."
—Rhonda Rich, *What Every Southern Woman Knows (that Every Woman Should)*

*T*HE FIRST THING OUTSIDERS NOTICE ABOUT Southerners is the way we talk. In fact, if it wasn't for our speech, some people wouldn't know a Southerner from a Minnesotan. And for a while there, that wasn't such a bad thing.

As late as the 1970s, almost every Southern man who wanted to be a success in business took language courses to lose his Southern accent. Southerners just weren't taken seriously by the rest of the country, and a Southern accent made businessmen assume you were a "tetch slow" (as we say in the South). Boy, have times changed. Not only is Atlanta a national center of business and Charlotte a center of banking, we've also put three of the last five Presidents in the White House—and they've all had Southern accents.

GRITS GLOSSARY

accent \ 'ak-,sent\ *n : a distinctive manner of pronunciation, especially local, that puts the kick into boring old speech. Especially prized when associated with the manner of speaking prevalent below the Mason-Dixon line.*

While Dixieland men may have struggled with a language inferiority complex, the opposite is true of Southern women. We've always known our accent is an asset, a special trait that makes us stand out from our Northern peers in all the best ways.

Whether it's a Mississippi drawl or a Tennessee twang, there is something about a Southern woman's accent that reminds us of the simple pleasures in life.

For one thing, men can't resist it. Our slow, musical speech drips with charm, and with the implied delights of a long, slow afternoon sipping home-brewed tea on the back porch.

GRITS GLOSSARY

South mouth \ 'saùth maùth\ *n : a loud mouth; enough said*

In educated circles, Southern speech is considered aristocratic, and for good reason: it is far closer linguistically to the Queen's English than any other American accent. Scottish, Irish, and rural English formed the basis of our language years ago, and the accent has held strong ever since. In the poor hill country there haven't been many other linguistic influences, and in Charleston you'd be hard pressed to tell a British tourist from a native.

GRITS GLOSSARY

drawl \'drȯl\ *v* : *to speak slower than average while prolonging a word's vowels; not to be confused with the drunken slurring of cowboys, a drawl is a beautiful thing to hear*

In the Delta of Mississippi and Louisiana, the mixture of French, West Indian, and Southern formed two dialects— Cajun and Creole—that in some places are far more like French than English.

How We Say It in the South

*E*ven without our accents, there are ways to pick out a Girl Raised in the South. If you hear any of the following, you'll know you have a Grits on your hands:

Busy as a one-armed paperhanger
(Durn busy)

Well, shut my mouth!
(Well, I declare!)

Well, I declare!
(I never woulda thunk it!)

Better than snuff and not near as dusty
(T'ain't bad.)

Nervous as a long-tailed cat in a room full of rocking chairs
(Durn nervous)

So ugly she'd run a dog off a meat wagon, bless her heart
(Durn ugly, poor thing)

A whistlin' woman and a crowin' him never come to
a good end.
(Don't go puttin' on airs.)

Be like the old lady who fell off the wagon.
(Ain't none o' your business, so get out.)

Kiss my grits.
(Kiss my unmentionables.)

Slow as molasses in January
(Slow as tar in December)

The Appalachian dialect of the mountains of West Virginia, Kentucky, and Tennessee is linguistically closer to Elizabethan English (the language of Shakespeare) than any other dialect spoken today. That includes the dialect spoken by the British royal family!

In other areas, the slave trade brought the rhythms of a thousand African languages, melding them into the musical coastal accents we can still hear today.

Yes, the Southern accent is as old as the hills—or at least the tobacco plantations of Northern Virginia—and just as varied. In fact, there are twenty-one different identified dialects in the South, including Carolina Mountain, Virginia Tidewater, South Carolina Low, Gullah, and Gumbo. (That last one's from the Delta, in case you hadn't guessed.)

And that's not to mention the other divisions within Southern speech. In cities like Atlanta that have recently welcomed citizens from as far away as Boston, Seattle, and China, many people have all but lost their Southern accents.

Southern Grammar Lesson

1. "Y'all" is singular.
2. "All y'all" is plural.
3. "All y'all's" is plural possessive.

Some African-American Southerners have returned to their roots, cultivating speech patterns based on inner-city street slang and the language of the slaves. In many cases, they have turned this dialect into art, producing some of the South's most important music, spoken words, poetry, and literature.

Then there's Society Speech and Country Club Chatter—those codes, motions, and sly comebacks that have developed over the last few decades in neighborhoods like Buckhead (Atlanta), Mountain Brook (Birmingham), and Belle Meade (Nashville). Grits using Society Speech may address one another as *Sugah, Sugah Lump, Precious, Darlin', Dumplin',* or *Sweet Pea.* We think these nicknames would be endearing just about anywhere.

GRITS GLOSSARY

society speech \ sə-'sī-ə-tē 'spēch\ *n* : *the manner of speaking you're likely to hear at the bridge tournament, the country club swimming pool, and the poshest hair salons*

There's one last thing you need to know about a Southern accent: there's no way to fake it. Speech is the spice of life in Dixie, and we take it very seriously. If you are not born below the Mason-Dixon line... honey, don't even try! No one outside the South can clone a version of the "dialect"-able form of communication that's such a part of Grits style. The only way to acquire a Southern accent is to hear one—over and over, from genuine Southern natives. So, y'all come on down.

If you can't say Darlin' like you mean it, sugah, just don't say anything at all.

CHAPTER 5

Pretty Is as Pretty Does:

The Grits Guide to Manners

*"Good manners are free, but
forgetting them often costs you dearly."*
—Traditional Southern Wisdom

$\mathcal{P}$ERHAPS THE MOST BASIC INGREDIENT TO a Girl Raised in the South is proper etiquette. Why is etiquette so important? Because good manners are a powerful tool. In some cases, in fact, they are the *most* powerful tool. They are the outward signs of our inner charm, and the intersection of femininity and style.

Manners are the rules that govern the behavior of a proper Southern woman—from our public demeanor to our style of

GRITS GLOSSARY

charm \ 'chärm\ *n : a power or quality of giving delight or arousing admiration; an attribute regularly seen in Girls Raised in the South.*

dress, from the way we hold a fork to the way we thank our hostess. Manners are important because they have been passed down to us from out mothers and grandmothers, all the way back as far as the family tree goes. They are a connection to the past, and reminder in this hectic age to slow down long enough to enjoy all the pleasures life has to offer.

Things weren't always as good in the South as they are now.

For most of our history, people received little formal education, work was backbreaking, and money was tight. Even in the most trying times Southern women's manners helped them maintain

> *When a Southern woman has nothing else,*
> *she still has her manners.*

a sense of pride, allowing them to hold their heads high even when their pockets were empty. Manners were something that could never be taken away by a bank, an unscrupulous boss, or the bad weather that often destroyed crops. Even if meals were meager, they were served with style and grace. Friends and strangers alike were greeted with kindness and decorum. And even if a woman had only one nice outfit, it would be washed, pressed, and ready for wearing on Sunday morning.

As hard as times have been on many Southern women, half of our sisters had it even worse. Long after slavery ended,

Southern girls know their mannered responses:

Yes, ma'am
Yes, sir
Why, no, Billy!

A Kentucky Grits Shows Her Class

*W*hen *Good Morning America* toured the South in the spring of 1999, Diane Sawyer—born and raised in Glasgow, Kentucky—proved that even a celebrity Grits sometimes has an off day. With cameras rolling, Ms. Sawyer stood up there in front of God and everybody, only to realize she had her pants on backward! Did this bona fide Southern celeb let that stop her from going on with the show? Of course not! She looked into the camera, laughed, and good-naturedly asked the world to please excuse her for having been in such a hurry that morning! Knowing how to keep cool under even the most embarrassing circumstances proved to us that even though she lives in New York, at heart Ms. Sawyer is still a Girl Raised in the South.

black Southern women weren't allowed even the basic freedoms of walking down the street, using a public rest room, or sending their children to public schools. In the face of cross burnings, stone throwing, and water hoses, it was the upbringing these Grits shared that helped them persevere. There is more power in a well-dressed woman who understands proper etiquette—even in the face of harassment—than there is in a world full of harassers. Just ask Rosa Parks, a paragon of dignity and manners who had the good sense to realize, at the right moment, that enough was enough.

We can all learn a lesson in manners from the women who make up the history of the South. After all, good breeding is our legacy. It's what being a Grits is all about!

GRITS PEARL OF WISDOM #5:

Southern women know it's improper to visit someone else's house without the proper outfit—especially the house of the Lord!

We don't have to tell you that getting caught saying something catty is one of the cardinal sins of Grits style. (That's getting *caught*, you hear?) Moreover, having had a few glasses of wine is no excuse. Grits never lose their heads over alcohol, a

When it comes to going out, a Girl Raised in the South . . .

- Never leaves home without "putting on her face"
- Knows her fashion limitations and sticks to them
- Has a versatile wardrobe, which covers every occasion and mood
- Never shows up for any occasion empty-handed
- Always demonstrates kindness and consideration—even when she doesn't feel like it
- Never forgets to send a thank-you note

Southern Traditions Are Grits Good

BY DARLENE REAL, ALABAMA GRITS

*E*very Sunday morning my mama—whom I was allowed only to call *Mother*—would get ready for church by placing her Sunday hat over her beautiful black hair, donning her gloves smartly, and picking up a matching handbag. My sister and I also had hats to put on and gloves to cover our little hands—Mother would have it no other way. My sister's gloves always seemed to have too few or too many fingers, making helping her get them on a funny-frustrating struggle.

We would have thought that Mother started this very prissy, tiresome custom herself, except that when we spent the summer with Grandmother she, too, had a hat, gloves, and matching handbag, even though she attended a one-room church. (My dear departed Grandmother never ever wore pants, and remains the only woman I've ever known to gather eggs in high heels.)

With this kind of tradition behind me, it's no wonder that when I roll out of bed in the morning, my mind immediately turns to my closet. While times have changed, I still feel the need to look smart—even for the carpool! My hat has been exchanged for a ball cap and my gloves left behind, but my handbag must still be appropriate and matching. My endearing mother and grandmother are alive through me, and their lessons have taught me well. No wonder some of my friends (and a few of my enemies) call me "Miss Priss"—after all, I'm a Girl Raised in the South.

> ## Southern Girls know the Three Deadly Sins:
>
> * Bad manners
> * Bad hair
> * Bad blind dates

man, or the good fortune of fellow Grits. That's not even manners: that's common sense.

Grits should never be caught in an embarrassing outfit because of poor planning. Accidents happen—a plate of ribs on your blouse or arriving at a party in the same dress as the hostess—but they should never happen because you didn't think ahead.

GRITS PEARL OF WISDOM #6:

If you can be ready to go in less than thirty minutes, you probably shouldn't be leaving the house at all!

Grits should always be charming and polite, as these are the keys to good manners. Always act as if your mother is watching, and never do anything you're going to be ashamed of the next day—unless it's just irresistible fun and doesn't hurt anyone but yourself, of course.

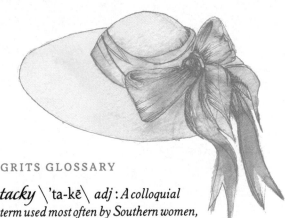

tacky \\'ta-kē\\ *adj* : *A colloquial term used most often by Southern women, describing a flagrant display of poor judgment in behavior or appearance. ex: "Did you see the hat Darla wore to the funeral? It's just too tacky to talk about."*

Grits know when enough is enough. Having good manners doesn't mean you should allow others to push you around. A Southern girl knows where to draw the line. (For those of you who are still learning, that's round about the third insult thrown your way by that neighbor who's had one too many mint juleps.)

In short, having Southern manners means conducting yourself with class at all times. Keep in mind that Grits should always be more composed than their men. After all, we're the

WELL, I DECLARE!:

Eighty percent of Southerners teach their children to say "ma'am" and "sir," compared to 46 percent of the rest of the country.

Not Your Stereotypical Southern Belle

BY BETSY SHEARON, GEORGIA GRITS

I grew up being more interested in scoring touchdowns than wearing tiaras. I never particularly wanted to get married and was well into my thirties before I even got engaged. And although I am a devoted aunt, the call of motherhood for me has always sounded strangely similar to the "Warning Will Robinson!" cry on the old *Lost in Space* television show.

Still, I consider myself a true Southern Girl, simply because, as we say in the South, my mama done raised me right. I say, "yes, ma'am," "no, sir," "please" and "thank you." I am respectful of my elders, even my great-aunt Ida Mable, whose food we were never allowed to eat at family reunions. (Suffice it to say that eccentricity not only runs in my family, it pretty much gallops.) I always wear clean underwear in case I am in an accident. And I always leave the house clean before I go on a trip in case I get killed and strangers have to come into my house to get my funeral wear (this is despite the fact that I have yet to read an obituary that said, "she left a husband, two children, and an immaculate house.")

And I know things that only Southern girls know, such as the fact that it is possible to "never talk to

continues...

strangers" and at the same time greet everyone you meet with a smile and a hello. I know that it is possible to "always tell the truth," but to always answer "fine" when someone asks how you are—even if your hair is on fire at the time. It is this knowledge that allows us to turn the other cheek when people say ugly things like "Southern girls are stupid, barefoot and pregnant." Southern girls realize that, given the swollen feet and ankles that accompany pregnancy, going barefoot when possible is actually a very smart and sensible thing to do—and that the Yankees who say things like that probably wouldn't talk so ugly if their feet didn't hurt, bless their hearts.

ones who are going to have to keep a cool head to straighten out the messes they get themselves into, bless their pea-pickin' hearts.

GRITS PEARL OF WISDOM #7:

Never do anything you wouldn't want published in your local newspaper.

Of course, there are certain rules that a Grits girl never has to be told—honey, she just *knows* that any of these faux pas will drop her straight into society's gutter. For those of you who are still learning, please pay close attention to this list of nevers, lest you find yourself on the wrong side of the social tracks:

- Never drink straight out of a beer can or bottle.
- Never walk down the street with a lighted cigarette.
- Never date your best friend's ex.
- Never be impolite to a police officer.
- Never wear white after Labor Day.
- Never wear different-colored polish on your toes than you're wearing on your fingers.
- Never cross your legs at the knees, always at the ankles.
- Never talk about age, real hair color, how much you paid for something, or how many times you've been married.
- Never pry into embarrassing family details (not openly, at least)

How to Write a Thank-You Note

1. Use the finest-grade stationery you can afford.
2. Remember that "thank you" is *two* words.
3. Always handwrite your note in ink, never ball-point or pencil.
4. Be specific when expressing why you are grateful.
5. Add a gracious, well-chosen closure. Options include:

    Warmly,
    Sweetly,
    Lovingly,
    Very Sincerely,
    Southernly,

Always put the note in the next day's post!

All this talk of manners should not lead you to believe that Grits are expected to be perfect—mercy, no! Girls Raised in the South are human, just like the rest of the world. In fact, we learn early on that if we can laugh and learn from our mistakes, we can even find inspiration in our foibles.

If you make a mistake in your manners, don't worry. You're safe among true Grits, because it's the worst manners of all to point out someone else's faults in public.

The most important thing to remember about manners is that actions speak louder than words.

CHAPTER 6

I Do Believe You Ate My Salad:

The Grits Guide to Table Manners

"Growing up I learned that social graces were often emphasized over achievement. There was so much focus on being a lady. In the South, where manners and behavior are very important, we were tamed early on."
—Sela Ward, Mississippi Grits

HE RULES WOMEN PLAY BY IN SOCIETY TODAY are drastically different than they were just a few years ago. For some, the art of being a Grits has been lost in the rush to become a self-sufficient, straight-shooting, aggressive survivor in the world. The fast way of life has been creeping slowly into our Southern way of doing things—especially dining. Breakfast, lunch, and dinner can so easily be acquired by drive through, ordering in, or buying prepared foods, that many of us Grits never put on an apron. (The closest some of our girlfriends come to whipping up a batch of grits is putting

GRITS GLOSSARY

cattywampus \ 'ka-tē 'wäm-pəs \ *adj : the direction the tablecloth is when it's not on the table straight. ex: "If you tuck the tablecloth into your pants and then get up to powder your nose, the tablecloth will go all cattywampus."*

on their Girls Raised in the South T-shirts!) Some seem to think that gives them a free pass to forget their table manners. Nothing could be further from the truth.

As Grits, we've been taught that one's behavior at the table reveals more about character than anything else. It must set us apart from the animals! Meals aren't just about eating; they're a time for sharing knowledge, events, plans, and relationships. Good company, food, and conversation can be enjoyed much more when using correct table manners and etiquette.

Mastering the basics of table manners is not difficult. Once mastered, you will be able to handle any dining situation, from

A Mother's Advice

Manners matter, regardless of your position in society. There is no excuse in this world to practice bad manners, especially at the table. I found that out in high school. I was invited to my boyfriend's house for dinner. His parents were somewhat formal, and I knew the dinner would be "fancy," at least in my mind. My family wasn't upper class (or even middle class), and my mother never had what would be called "social graces."

Before I left, my mother gave me a piece of advice: hold your head high, be quiet, and take the lead from his mother. Even though I was scared to death, I did what my mother advised and got through the experience with flying colors.

To this day, my mother's advice has gotten me though many difficult situations, especially ones that are totally new to me! With my mother's simple advice, I know I could dine with the Queen of England, just by following her lead. Thanks, Mother!

—Deborah Ford

Mirror Magic

BY NORMA HARTMAN,

ARKANSAS GRITS

My mother, Thelma Louise Lee Hedgepeth, grew up in Brookhaven, Mississippi. She had three children and seven grandchildren.

Every Sunday after church we would go to her house for a lovely lunch with all of her serving pieces fully displayed. It was very important for her family to know exactly how to present themselves, especially at the table. Even though her china, crystal, and silverware may not have matched, they were properly placed around each place setting.

Mother went to Fred's Dime Store and bought enough mirrors to place in front of all of her children and grandchildren's plates so we all could see exactly how we looked while eating. She spent time making sure we used the correct utensils and held them properly, and, of course, paid attention to how we put the food in our mouths. The mirror never lied! She always told us that how we act in public—especially how we eat—would be extremely important all our lives.

the most casual to the most formal, with graciousness and poise. The purpose of nearly every aspect of table manners is to preserve cleanliness and proper appearance.

Take the oft-abused napkin, for example. A true Grits takes

great care not to soil any part of the table linen—including the napkin. Unless they're eating barbeque or watermelon, Southern girls make every attempt to keep the napkin in pristine condition throughout the course of the meal. That's fine linen, honey, not your lipstick-removal system!

Treat a napkin with respect. First, remove it from the place setting, unfold it, and place it gently in your lap. When you use it, be delicate: dab at your lips, don't smear them. Never crumple your napkin; instead, fold it carefully away from you, so that the crumbs don't fall back on your lap. When you leave the table at the end of the meal, leave your napkin next to your plate, not under it—and *never* on your chair.

Southern girls know how to eat watermelon on a hot summer day:

Plenty of napkins...
Plenty of salt...
And, darlin', leave your good clothes at home!

Of course, the most important aspect of the meal is the eating itself. At smaller events, it is common to wait to take a bite until everyone at the table has received a serving and the hostess has begun eating. At larger events, the hostess may urge her guests to eat immediately upon receiving the food.

WELL, I DECLARE!:

Every Grits knows that a paper cup is called a "Dixie cup," but did you know that this name has nothing to do with Dixieland proper? In fact, the very first Dixie brand cup was produced in 1908 by two men in Boston, Massachusetts. (We've got to give those Yankees credit for realizing that the key to success is a Southern name!) Marketed as the "Health Kup," this invention helped abolish the widespread but unsanitary practice of keeping common cups near public water receptacles. Today, Grits have adopted the brand name to mean any disposable cup.

At formal gatherings, you're going to encounter some pretty complex table settings. Don't get your panties in a twist! Dealing with any table setting is so easy it can't go wrong, unless the table was improperly set to start with. The rule is this: begin with the outermost utensils and move inward. In a formal place setting, you will receive exactly as much silverware as you will need, arranged in precisely the right order. The silverware will be removed with the used dish, and in some cases new silverware will be brought to you after you have finished the previous course.

American vs. Continental

(And no, we're not talking about airlines, honey!)

The Continental Style vs. the American Style of utensil use is one of the great debates in the world of manners. While we are as patriotic as Americans get, we also can't forget that many Southerners trace their roots all the way back to the European continent. And while some might say that the Continental style looks lowbrow, we should all keep in mind that our system of place setting makes the Continental style the more logical choice. So in the end, we think *you* should be the one to decide. As long as you look like you know what you're doing and never, ever eat directly off your knife, either of the following methods is acceptable:

American Style: Hold the fork in your left hand and the knife in your right. After cutting, lay the knife down with the blade on the right side of your plate, and switch the fork to the right hand to eat. At the end of your meal, your utensils should be balanced together on the right side of the plate.

Continental Style: Hold the fork in your left hand, tines curved down, and the knife in your right hand. You do not need to put down your knife to eat off your fork. At the end of the meal, the blade of the knife and the tines of the fork should be crossed over each other on the center of the plate.

The Dos and Don'ts of Grits Table Manners

Do...

...unfold the napkin on your lap as soon as you sit down

...wait for your host or hostess to start eating before digging in

...pick up your napkin if you drop it

...pass serving plates to the right

...try a little bit of every-thing

...take your time—no gulping or gobbling

...keep the table around your plate as clean as possible

...say, "Excuse me for a moment, please" if you need to leave the table

...say "Please" and "Thank you"

...tip graciously—that's at least 17 percent, ladies

Do not...

...come to a table with gum in your mouth (to be safe, don't *ever* chew gum)

...take a cell phone or pager into a dining situation

...put your elbows on the table (were you born in a barn?)

...drink through a straw

...slurp, burp, or make any noise with your food

...reach over someone's plate to get something

...divorce the salt and pepper shakers—always pass them both, no matter which was requested

...ever, ever, ever (are we clear?) use a toothpick

...leave the table until all are finished

Formal Table Setting

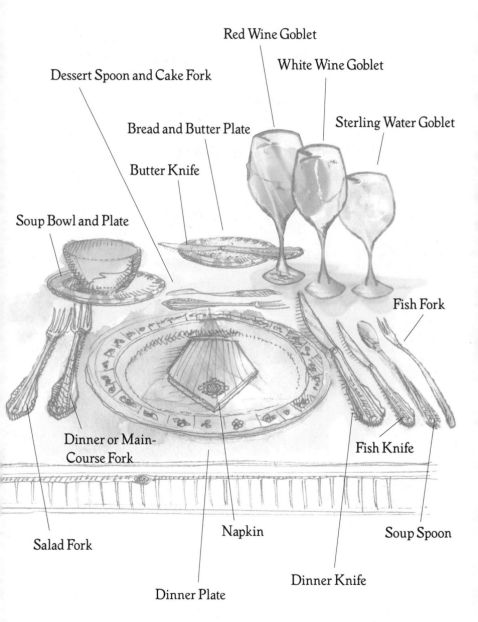

Red Wine Goblet

White Wine Goblet

Dessert Spoon and Cake Fork

Sterling Water Goblet

Bread and Butter Plate

Butter Knife

Soup Bowl and Plate

Fish Fork

Dinner or Main-Course Fork

Fish Knife

Salad Fork

Napkin

Soup Spoon

Dinner Plate

Dinner Knife

Informal Table Setting

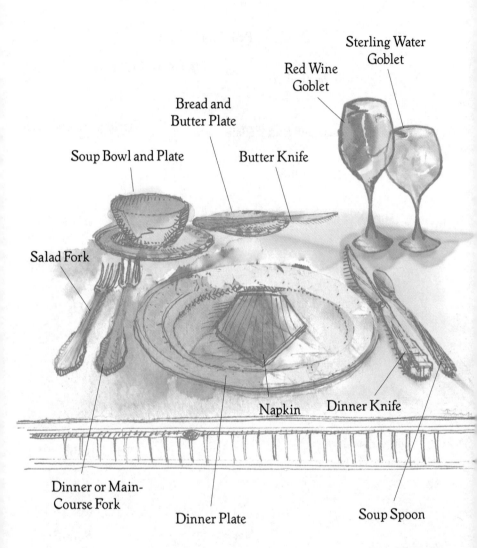

Sterling Water Goblet

Red Wine Goblet

Bread and Butter Plate

Butter Knife

Soup Bowl and Plate

Salad Fork

Napkin

Dinner Knife

Dinner or Main-Course Fork

Dinner Plate

Soup Spoon

A Grits Guide to the Finger Bowl*

After a fancy meal requiring the use of one's fingers, it is polite to present your guests with a finger bowl for touching up their digits before dessert. Guests should dip their fingertips in the water (absolutely no scrubbing) and dry them with their napkins. The bowl should then be set to the side of the plate to be collected by the hostess before the final course arrives.

Not to be confused with Peach, Iron, Cotton, and/or Sugar Bowls!

More important than identifying silverware is knowing how to use it. True Southern girls have been raised to use their utensils properly. In fact, we've just about got it down to an art form.

- Always hold your silverware delicately, using your fingertips as a guide.
- The spoon and fork should be held horizontally by balancing them between the first knuckle of the middle finger and the tip of the index finger, using the thumb to steady the handle.
- Gently press the tip of your index finger over the top of the knife blade, using it as a guide as you cut.
- Used flatware must never be allowed to touch the surface of the table.
- Food items and drinks like tea and coffee are usually

presented with a plate underneath the bowl or cup, on which the utensil must be placed after use.

- Flatware should always be placed on the plate as you pause between bites.

WELL, I DECLARE!:

Did you know that the fork was first invented in ancient China, but quickly became obsolete in favor of the more popular chopsticks? It's no surprise to us Grits—we've always known that two is better than one.

Watermelon is a quintessential Southern summer food, whether served on the lawn, at the local diner, or sitting in the country club. It's also a Sunday-best danger, because no sort of food stain—not even that endearingly telltale pink watermelon spot—is an acceptable accessory to your lightly starched cotton sundress. It's not a question of whether to partake of the fruit or not: watermelon is tradition, and nowhere in the South can it go uneaten! But learn these simple watermelon rules, and there's no reason your afternoon picnic needs to turn into a fashion tragedy:

1. Be prepared whenever watermelon is a possibility! There's room for a hankie in even the smallest Sunday handbag.
2. Never eat watermelon standing up.
3. In public, watermelon is best eaten with a fork. If none is available, and the fruit must be bitten directly off the

I Do Believe
You Ate My Salad

*R*ecently, I attended a luncheon at the George Lindsey (Goober of Mayberry fame) Film Festival at my alma mater, the University of North Alabama. Good manners and polite social behavior were at the top of my list, for I know how often business deals get made and people fall in love over meals—my goodness!

Seated right next to me was my friend Buddy Killen, a legendary songwriter from Nashville, Tennessee. Everything seemed to be going fine until I looked over and saw that Buddy was eating my salad. I guess he forgot that your salad is always served on the right.

Should I have ignored his faux pas? Skipped my salad to avoid making him uncomfortable? What was a Grits girl to do?

I'll tell you what: without a second thought, I turned to Buddy and said straight out, "Excuse me, sir, I do believe you ate my salad!" Never missing a beat, he waved the waiter over and said, "Sir, I'm afraid you forgot Edie's salad!"

With that, I got my salad and all honor was saved. Which just goes to show that being straightforward in a polite manner is never inappropriate.

—Edie Hand

rind, be sure to hold it delicately and lean slightly forward as you eat.

4. Never spit your seeds. Remove them from your mouth gracefully with your fork, or discreetly with your napkin.

NOTE: None of the above rules apply when you and your girlfriend bust one open in the melon patch. When you're having that much fun, anything goes!

A Southern girl knows that beauty can fade and wealth can leave her, but her character is a lasting legacy. Being called a "Southern lady" and obeying all the requisite manners is perhaps the highest compliment a Grits can receive. It's all in the presentation, sugah.

Reminder: good table manners are the ultimate symbol of who you are, and how you were raised.

CHAPTER 7

Thank the Lord for Answered Prayers:

The Grits Guide to Getting Your Man

*"Someday we'll tell our kids, until you
find love like this, don't settle for anything less."*
—LeAnn Rimes, country music star and Texas Grits, on
her marriage to Dean Sheremet

"I thought I told you to stay in the car."
—Tallulah Bankhead, legendary Alabama Grits, on seeing
a former boyfriend for the first time in years

$\mathscr{F}$INDING AND KEEPING A LIFELONG PARTNER is a common dream of all girls, everywhere. Women love men (well, most of us, anyway—Ellen DeGeneres is a Louisiana Grits, after all!), and Grits are no exceptions. We think about true love as much as the next girl—maybe more, thanks to that romantic Southern atmosphere.

Finding a man is like eating a meal: it's tasty, it's tempting, and it keeps you alive. Sometimes it's bad for you, sometimes it goes down wrong, but the most important thing is that you've tried everything on your plate. And once it's gone, there is simply no use in worrying about it. Go ahead and try to exercise off the effects, but remember: there's another one coming down the road, and it's going to be better (or at least more tempting) than the last. So tie on that napkin, darlin', and get ready to dig in!

Men are important to Southern girls,
but they don't define us.

Reunion

*T*hank god we get second chances. I was blessed to find my Right Man, Mark, after thirteen years of being a single mom. Our story begins in a rural northwest Alabama town set like a novel. My high school business teacher saw me at a funeral, of all places, and said, "Edie, do you remember Mark Aldridge?" Of course I remembered: thirty years earlier Mark had been captain of the high school football team, while I was the head cheerleader. People always thought of us together, but we only had one date—senior prom—before setting off to make our dreams come true at different universities. Now, two weeks after seeing Mrs. Cashion, Mark and I were having coffee and conversation about his children and my son. Wow! He looked great...and such a gentleman. As we were leaving, Mark popped the big question: "Will you go with me to our thirty-year class reunion?" I knew when Mark picked me up at my aunt Clyneice's that he was the Right Man. We married two years later under a tent at a celebrity golf tournament I had organized, with friends and family all around. Love is a beautiful thing.

—Edie Hand

If you're single and you're not having the greatest fun of your life, it's high time to reassess your priorities. It may be hard to see it, but these are the carefree spring days in the seasons of your life! Enjoy them. Be your own person. Be

The Right Men

- Daddy
- Jimmy Carter
- Martin Luther King, Jr.
- Andy Griffith
- Daddy
- Robert E. Lee
- Samuel L. Jackson
- Peyton Manning
- Daddy

happy. Be confident. If you've heard it once, you've heard it a thousand times: nothing attracts a man like confidence. And if that doesn't work, don't be afraid to chase him down like a greased pig at the county fair. It's long past the time when it wasn't acceptable for a woman to make the first move, after all. And make sure he knows your attention is precious: he'd better use it or lose it. If *that* doesn't work, he's probably just one of those slow types, bless his heart, and you're better off without him.

GRITS PEARL OF WISDOM #10:

Only agree to marry a man who loves you more than you love him. If he doesn't love you like he means it now, he never will.

If, on the other hand, you're in a relationship and you're not having a good time, honey, it's time to hit the road. Don't let that dream package—dress, ring, cake, ceremony, handsome man, children—turn into a blindfold. As Grits, instinct is our greatest asset. You know it when you're getting less than you

How to Flirt, Southern Style

♥ Smile while holding eye contact. It makes you appear approachable.

♥ Never cross your arms, or you'll send the message that he's not welcome.

♥ Flutter your eyelashes.

♥ Notice something special. Remember: flattery will get you *everywhere*.

♥ Put yourself in a target position—in the center of the room, not hidden away in a corner.

♥ Wear the right color. Pinkish peach is a known man magnet.

♥ Use the right scent. Men love vanilla or cinnamon. It reminds them of dessert.

♥ Be a good listener, but play hard to get.

♥ Be yourself and, for god's sake, have fun!

deserve, and there's no teaching old dogs new tricks. If he's not putting up, it's *you* who should be shutting up—shutting up shop and movin' on to the next town, that is!

The right Southern man knows that a kitchen appliance is never, ever an appropriate birthday gift.

Your Right Man is out there, waiting—you just have to know where to look. It's a challenge, but it's just about the most fun you're ever going to have. Remember, he's as anxious as you are. If not, there's something wrong with him already.

A Note on Logistics

- *Where to meet a man:* church, grocery store, video store, gym, bookstore, wedding, class reunion, traffic accident, sporting event—just about anywhere and everywhere

- *Where not to meet a man:* prison, divorce court, a dark alley (unless it's a bowling alley, and even that's a bit questionable)

The Southern Girl

BY SAMUEL ALFRED BEADLE

(1857–1932)

The fairest thing on land or sea
Is the Southern girl, to me.
You should see her when the stars
Come studding all the sky;
And feel her beaming eye
On you when the moon is full—
Fairest of all that's fair is she,
The Southern girl, to me.

So, how do you know when you meet the Right Man?
Here are some hints:

• **The right Southern man knows chivalry isn't dead.**
Good manners should be a part of a Southern man's genes.

GRITS PEARL OF WISDOM #9:

The right Southern man knows how to
BBQ, and he does it without question. A
Southern woman never cooks outside.

Listen up, Southern mamas: it's up to *you* to raise your sons right. Don't forget this obligation to your fellow Grits!

• **The right Southern man is one of a kind.** He reveres his ancestors, adores his children, puts his wife and his mother on a pedestal, savors his cocktail hour, shows infinite loyalty to his best friends, and knows his handshake is his word. What a gentleman!

• **The right Southern man has the right hobbies.** Please, girls, remember that a Southern man is expected to hunt, fish, play golf, work on cars, and watch sports on television. We do want manly men! However, if your significant other starts to forget birthdays or other important dates because of a car race or a hunting trip, that's a sure sign of trouble. And if he starts to act tacky, like giving you earrings made from fishing lures for your birthday, it's time to draft that personal ad.

Are these expectations too high? Mercy, no. Southern girls have high expectations for themselves, and their expectations should be just as high for their men. Remember that old saying: until you know and love yourself, there's no hoping to find a man that'll do it for you.

Looking for a man, or *courting*, as we like to call it down here, may be a lot of fun—remember, girls, *it's a lot of fun*—but

GRITS GLOSSARY

The Rock \thə' räk\ *n : the true sign of a man's love, and of his pocketbook; Southern girls know the importance of the 4 Cs: cut, clarity, carat... and cost.*

> ## A Southern girl knows the importance of a real man:
>
> Man*icures*
> Man*ors*
> Man*ners*
> Man*ipulation*
> Many man*ly men!*

like everything else in the South it comes with a very formal tradition. Courtship doesn't have to be done the old-fashioned way, but if you want the full Southern experience, you better make sure your man follows this simple progression:

• **Flowers and candy.** Gifts are the first step to a serious relationship. You aren't in this for nothing, now! *If a man doesn't understand you enough to know the gifts you want after two months, he might be a Reject.*

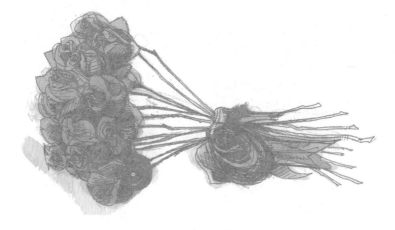

• **Lavalier.** In the dictionary, a lavalier is a jeweled pendant worn on a chain around the neck. In Southern dating circles, it's any pin or nice piece of jewelry that symbolizes that this relationship is getting serious. *If your man gives you something he got free from Marlboro, he might be a Reject.*

• **Promise ring.** This is just what it sounds like. It's a ring, symbolizing the promise to be married—a formal engagement to be engaged. Once you've got a promise ring, you're joined to your man at the hip—or at least the finger. *If he still refuses to let you meet his mother, he might be a Reject.*

Calling Mr. Wrong!

Here are some sure signs the man you're seeing is headed down the wrong set of tracks:

- He calls his mama more than he calls you
- He asked your sister, cousin, friend or recently divorced aunt for a date
- He doesn't have a job
- He says he has no family
- He doesn't like dogs
- He looks in the mirror more than you do
- You call *that* a kiss?

• **Engagement ring.** A romantic engagement is nice, but not necessary. *We'd all love to get engaged at the beach, or in a remote cabin in the Smoky Mountains, but as long as he's down on one knee and produces a rock—a real rock, not something cubic he got off television—then he might just be a Keeper.*

After the Wedding ...

• Relax, relax, relax, and enjoy that honeymoon!

• Don't panic if it takes some time to adjust to being married—it can take up to a year to find your marriage "sea legs."

• Talk about feelings with your husband, not your friends.

• Set aside time to be alone when you need it.

• Have a date once a week (with your husband, of course).

• Learn to pick your battles—remember, marriage is about compromise.

• Schedule time with the girls, and allow him time with the boys.

• Don't sweat the small stuff—Grits don't sweat ... we glisten!

• **The wedding band.** Men don't understand weddings, which is why we have a separate chapter on the big event. *As long as he shows up, sober, with the ring, he's a Keeper.*

I Do ... Adieu?

A mistake is nothing to be ashamed of, even if it does set the neighborhood tongues a-waggin'! Just take a look at this list of Southern women who've said "I Do" to at least two:

- Julia Roberts, Georgia Grits (twice)
- Amy Grant, Georgia/Tennessee Grits (twice)
- Faith Hill, Mississippi Grits (twice)
- Deborah Ford, Alabama Grits (four times, but the first didn't count: God and my mama annulled that one!)

Now, Southern women know that wrangling the Right Man doesn't signal the end of the game—or the fun, for heaven's sake. Grits are taught from birth to stand by their man. And as long as he treats us right, that's just what we'll do.

"To find the right man: Be selective, not restrictive—and for god's sake, explore!"

—Dr. Judy Karlansky, Kentucky Grits

ma'am \ 'mam\ *n : what we'll call your "Right Man", if he chooses to wear earrings, pierce his nose, and wear his hair long*

Trust, commitment, compatibility, cooperation, and compromise are key ingredients for a lasting relationship—romance is just the icing! Studies have shown that what women want most in their relationships is more romance. Well, if you're waiting for that old lug to put the romance into the relationship, you might as well try to win the Winston Cup in your brother's pickup—you're not even going to qualify, honey. He may be Mr. Right, but he's still a man, sugah! Southern girls know their love lives are doomed to boredom if they don't take matters into their own hands. Add a little spice, and a surprise here or there. Don't ever become ordinary—keep pampering your man, and make sure it comes back to you double in return.

"Charisma is the middle name
of scads of Southern cads."

—*Rosemary Daniel, Grits writer*

PART III

Southern Hospitality

CHAPTER 8

Slow Cookin'
and Cornbread:

The Grits Guide
to Southern Foods

*"Southerners can't stand to eat alone. If we're
going to cook a mess of greens we want to eat
them with a mess of people."*
—Julia Reed, Grits writer

*"My idea of heaven is a great big baked potato
and someone to share it with."*
—Oprah Winfrey, Mississippi Grits

$\mathscr{I}$F THERE'S ONE THING BESIDES OUR ACCENTS that Southerners are known and admired for, it's our cooking. Cooking in the South has always been about "comfort food"—slow cooked and hearty, featuring all the good things the land has to offer: pork (the *only* barbecue meat), corn, squash, collard greens, okra, and, of course, watermelon. The South is a feast, and Grits are always ready to dig in. And as we always remember, you don't have to cook it to know it and love it.

WELL, I DECLARE!:
Hush puppies are rumored to have gotten their name from hunters who threw the leftover ends of their cornbread to their dogs to keep them quiet at night.

Now, we've done some digging and we've discovered that the story of Southern food is just about as delicious as the food itself. This information may not help you become as fabulous a chef as Emeril Lagasse (let's be truthful—probably not even an *okay* one), but it will sure help you understand where our delicious cuisine comes from. And how many times do we have to say that it's all about heritage in the land of Grits?

For Grits girls, cooking is strictly optional.
That's what restaurants are for, honey!

Southern food begins with two staples of our region: corn and berries. Both were gifts from the Native Americans, and they were just about the only things that kept the early settlers alive. These pioneers weren't easily convinced that the South was for them; in fact, early coastal women rebelled when they were told they had to use cornmeal instead of white European

A Classic Grits Recipe for the Cooking-Challenged

1. Cook up some canned biscuits.
2. Pour chicken divan (from a can, of course) over biscuits.
3. Add a few sprigs of this and that, whatever is handy.

Of course, it's all presentation for the Southern belle. If it doesn't look like it's out of a can, how will he *evah* know?

Cracklin' Corn Bread

1 cup self-rising cornmeal
1 cup buttermilk
1 cup pork cracklin's
½ cup self-rising flour
¼ cup and 4 tablespoons vegetable oil

Preheat the oven to 450°. In a large mixing bowl, combine the cornmeal, buttermilk, cracklin's, flour, and ¼ cup of oil. In an 8-inch skillet, heat 4 tablespoons of oil on the stove until it is very hot. Pour the batter into the skillet. Transfer to the oven and bake 20 minutes or until golden brown, slice, and serve warm. Add a glass of hot tea and sliced onions and get set for the best 10 minutes of eating you'll do in the South!

Yield: 8 to 10 servings

flour. Just like all us opinionated Grits—we love our traditions and don't take kindly to being told what to do! Fortunately for us all, however, the absence of white flour meant that our settlers had to invent a new kind of bread. You guessed it—*cornbread*. They also invented grits, a porridge made from ground-up hominy corn. (It took a true Southern belle, though, to learn how to slather them in pepper and butter.)

The Okra Garden

*T*here are a lot of plants in a Southern garden—tomatoes, potatoes, greens, squash, and sometimes even melons—but the one that makes it a true *Southern* garden is okra. Okra likes warm, dry weather, but it will grow in most parts of the United States, so it's not a matter of environment, honey, it's a matter of TLC.

1. Plant okra seeds in spring, two to three weeks after the last frost.

2. Plant seeds one inch deep in the soil, two inches apart. You should leave three feet between rows of plants. When the seeds sprout, thin the plants to one foot apart.

3. Water okra once a week only—it loves dry soil.

4. Okra produces flowers after two months. About four days later, the okra pods will appear. They should be harvested when three to four inches long.

5. You're about to find out two very unpleasant things about okra. First, you have to hack the vegetable off the stalk with a knife. Second, the plant is fibrous and extremely itchy. Don't give up, darling! Okra is well worth the struggle.

6. Okra is best eaten fresh. It can be boiled, battered in cornmeal, or stewed in a gumbo. Corn battered is the classic method, but believe us, they're all good.

The next step toward the birth of our Southern cuisine was the introduction of pork. For that, we can thank the Spanish—or, more specifically, Spanish explorer Hernando de Soto. He traveled all over the South looking for treasure, and ended

Dolly Parton's Favorite Meat Loaf

  1½ pounds ground sirloin (or other lean meat)
  ½ cup ketchup
  ½ cup tomato juice
  2 eggs, beaten
  ¾ cup fresh bread crumbs
  ½ cup onions, finely chopped
  2 teaspoons prepared mustard
  ½ teaspoon salt
  ½ teaspoon pepper
  Green pepper and/or celery (optional)

Mix all ingredients with hands and put in baking dish. Bake at 400° about 1 hour (or until desired doneness). After baking for about 45 minutes, pour extra ketchup on top and continue to bake.

NOTE: Best served with mashed potatoes, creamed corn, and apple pie.

—Dolly Parton, Tennessee Grits

barbeque \ 'bär-bi-,kyü\ *n* : *pulled or chopped pork or ribs, marinated or specially seasoned to be cooked over an open fire; the only valid excuse for a Southern girl to lick her fingers in public*

up dying near the Mississippi River without a penny to his name. But the silver lining (for us, anyway) is that he left behind the pigs he'd brought with him, which would eventually be tamed and raised as the number one meat in the Southern diet. Thank goodness for that—where would the South be without country ham, thick slabs of side bacon, or that most central of Southern dishes, barbeque?

WELL, I DECLARE!:

Brunswick stew is a Southern version of chili that often accompanies barbeque. Created in the region around Brunswick, Georgia, original recipes featured squirrel and opossum meat as primary ingredients. (Nowadays, most of us just use pork or chicken.)

That brings us to a powerful misconception about barbeque among non-Southerners, which needs to be set right. In some places in the North, people take a roasted chicken and call it barbeque. In other places, the word *barbeque* can be used to describe anything cooked on a backyard grill.

As every Southerner knows, *barbeque* means only two things: pulled pork and ribs. Both have to be cooked slowly over a pit fire built with real wood for that great smoked flavor. The secret, of course, is the sauce, of which three have been officially recognized with the highest designation given in the South: "Deee-*licious!*"

· **Tomato-based sauce.** The classic red stuff, loaded with spices and dripping with goodness.
· **Vinegar-based sauce.** Clear, tart, and especially popular in North Carolina.
· **Mustard-based sauce.** Often associated with South Carolina, this spicy yellowish sauce is a wild card served to unsuspecting customers in chop joints in every region of the South. Once they get over the shock, though, must customers agree that mustard makes for some darn good pig.

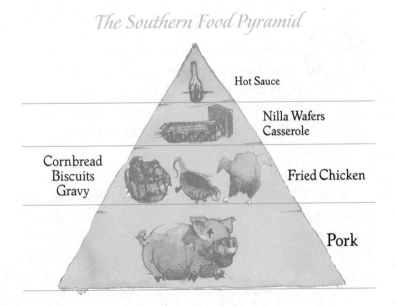

The Southern Food Pyramid

Hot Sauce

Nilla Wafers
Casserole

Cornbread
Biscuits
Gravy

Fried Chicken

Pork

Basic Gumbo Filé

1 quartered onion
3 quarts water
½ bell pepper
salt and pepper
3 garlic cloves
shrimp, oysters (½ pound each)
3 tablespoons bacon grease
1 teaspoon filé seasoning
3 tablespoons flour

Let the onion, garlic, and bell pepper simmer in the water until very soft. Remove, reserving the water, mash, and discard the pepper skin. Return the pulp to the water. Make a dark roux of the bacon grease and flour. Slowly stir the roux into the water, adding salt and pepper. Cook 5 minutes, add oysters and shrimp, and simmer 5 more minutes. After the gumbo is removed from the heat, add the filé just before serving.

Yield: 4 servings

—*River Road Recipes,* Junior League of Baton Rouge

Now, ladies, you must be careful with barbeque—outside of watermelon, there isn't a messier food south of the Mason-Dixon line. That's why Grits are given a free pass to get their fingers dirty on a good piece of barbeque. Just keep it off your dress, now, and don't forget our instructions for the proper use of a finger bowl (see p. 59).

The final touches to Southern cuisine came with the introduction of collard greens, okra, peas, yams, watermelon, and

GRITS PEARL OF WISDOM #12:

Don't ever plant a watermelon within thirty feet of a squash, zucchini, or cucumber. The plants will crossbreed and results will be ugly. Unless you like hard yellow watermelon and watery pink squash, that is.

peanuts. These staples came over with the millions of Africans brought to America as slaves. Southerners have lived off of them ever since.

It's not just the ingredients that make Southern foods Southern, it's the way we cook them. Southern cooking is as laid back as our lifestyle. You can't rush quality, after all. Southern-style ribs and pork chops are cooked on low heat for hours. Real Southern fried chicken is batter dipped and left to season overnight. A true Southerner will cook collard greens for three to four days at a very low temperature in a big old iron skillet, stirring occasionally, until all the bitterness drains away.

The water left behind, called "pot liquor," is used to flavor meals later on.

Now, some people will ask: with all these vegetables, surely you've got some vegetarian Grits down there? Well, not to put down the vegetable eaters among us, but there's just no such thing as a real Southern vegetarian. That's because everything in the South is seasoned with the same thing: pork. What makes collard greens so tasty? It's the hunk of pork fat that simmers in the pot. Battered okra, a true Southern delicacy, is only done right when cooked in animal fat. Same goes for fried green tomatoes. And gravy, after all, is just pork fat and flour.

GRITS GLOSSARY

Southern vegetarian \ 'sə-thərn, ve-jə'ter-ē-ən\ *n :poor soul.*

Even cornbread can be made with cracklin's, the hard, crispy bits of fat that float in the skillet after chicken or pork has been cooked. In fact, you can still buy cracklin' fat—hand-tied in a plastic bag and ready to fry—in most traditional soul food markets, like Atlanta's Sweet Auburn Market. So do

A Southern Vegetarian's Story

BY ERIN STEWART, ALABAMA GRITS

It wasn't easy being a vegetarian in Huntsville, Alabama, but I managed it throughout my high school years. At least I thought I did. I remember one trip with my parents that threw everything into doubt.

It was a Saturday, and we had reservations at Miss Mary Bobo's, the famous restaurant in Lynchburg, Tennessee, the home of Jack Daniel's whiskey. Miss Mary Bobo's is known for serving at least one item cooked in Jack Daniel's at every meal: this time it was the apples. What really interested me, though, was the greens. I think they were mustard greens. I was just eating my third bite when a large man next to me turned to our hostess, who was watching us all eat at one communal table, and said, "Miss Mary Bobo, these are the best greens I've ever had. What's your secret?"

Without a second thought, she replied, "Why, real lard, of course." I must confess: I took one more bite before I put my fork down! (Don't tell anyone!) To this day, those are some of the best greens I've ever tasted.

yourself a favor: go get yourself some classic Southern fatback before it's all gone.

CHAPTER 9

Southern Girls Don't Drink:

The Grits Guide to Drinking

"I know folks all have a tizzy about it, but I like a little bourbon of an evening. It helps me sleep. I don't much care what they say about it."
—Lillian Carter, Georgia Grits

"Always go home before you forget your mother-in-law's real name."
—Southern Girl Saying

$\mathcal{S}$OUTHERNERS HAVE LEGENDARY THIRSTS. Maybe it's the high heat and humidity, or maybe it's the fact that we love to socialize over a cold glass of tea or a nice splash of bourbon and branch. We've created our own drinks, from Coca-Cola to bourbon whiskey, and our own unique way of enjoying them. In fact, you could say drinking is a way of life in the South—and we're not just talking about alcohol. But whatever kind of beverage we're holding, one thing is always true: Southern women don't drink—we sip... a lot! That's Southern girl style.

Sipping, for Grits, means:

- Mimosas (in the morning)
- Lemonade (in the heat)
- Iced tea (at lunch)
- Wine (whenever its "whine" time)
- Beer (but only in a glass, of course)
- Cocktails (whenever the occasion calls for them)
- Coke (when we've had too much of the last three)

Old-Fashioned Lemonade

12 lemons
3 cups of sugah
5 quarts of water
Lots of ice cubes!

Slice 4 lemons thinly and set aside. Roll each of the remaining lemons, unpeeled, against the countertop with the palm of your hand to release their juices. Slice each lemon in half and squeeze juice into a large pitcher. Add water and sugar; stir until sugar is dissolved. Add sliced lemons. Pour lemonade into tall glasses full of ice, and enjoy!

Yield: 20 eight-ounce servings

GRITS PEARL OF WISDOM #13:

If anyone tries to tell you a Southern girl shouldn't drink, just tell them the truth: we don't drink, we sip . . . a lot.

If you're going to talk about drinks in the South, you have to start with iced tea. Now, a lot of Northerners have gotten the wrong impression about this Southern tradition. They seem to think it's just hot tea with ice in it—*cold* tea in other words—and that you can bottle it, flavor it, and sell it out of a cooler. Do we even need to tell you that stuff's not *real* iced tea, sugah?

There are only two kinds of Southern iced tea: sun tea and sweet tea. Sun tea is warmed and brewed by the sun. Sweet tea's a little more complex. Even in some places in the South these days, you get served a sweet tea that is just iced tea with

Sun Tea: The House Wine of the South

3 tea bags
1 quart cold water

Put the tea bags into a clear glass quart jar filled with water. Set in the sun for several hours until the tea is nice and warm. Sweeten to your taste—but don't you dare call it sweet tea.

Yield: 1 quart

sugar in it. What a disgrace! That's no more sweet tea than a basset hound is a coon dog.

Now, listen up, because making great sweet tea is something all Grits must know. It's not that hard, honey, it just takes patience, that wonderful trait all us Southern girls are known for.

WELL, I DECLARE!:

Iced tea was first introduced at the 1904 St. Louis World's Fair. A South Carolina–grown tea won the "Best in Show" medal.

Sweet tea starts with hot tea, right off the stove. Don't make it too hot, now—that will ruin the flavor. While the tea is still hot, *slowly* pour in the sugar. It's got to be hot or the sugar won't dissolve right, which is the part most people don't understand. Once the sugar is dissolved, take that tea out to the patio and let it cool slowly. Once it's room temperature, pour the sweet tea over ice and you've got yourself the perfect glass of real Southern refreshment.

GRITS PEARL OF WISDOM #14:

Nothing too easy, or done too quickly, is going to be right. It takes time to create perfection, whether it's your tea or your hair.

While the South may love its tea, we're probably best known for another nonalcoholic concoction: soda pop. Not that true Grits would ever use that term. Grits always refer to these drinks as cokes, whether they're Coca-Cola or not.

GRITS GLOSSARY

coke \ 'kōk\ *n* : *denotes any carbonated beverage, regardless of brand name*

Hostess: *"What you want to drink, precious?"*
Guest: *"What kind of coke you got?"*
Hostess: *"We got Coke, Diet Coke, Dr Pepper, and Mountain Dew."*
Guest: *"Hmmm. I think I'll have a Coke, please."*

Real Grits always order the same kind of coke—diet!

WELL, I DECLARE!:

Old-timers in the South had a special way of drinking their Royal Crown Cola (better known as RC): they would pour salted peanuts into the RC bottle before drinking.

I'd Like to Buy the South a Coke . . .

The South truly is the home of coke (or soda to Northerners), as this list of famous and infamous brands born South of the Mason-Dixon line proves:

- Ale-8-One (Winchester, Kentucky)
- Barq's Root Beer (Biloxi, Mississippi)
- Big Red (Waco, Texas)
- Cheerwine (Salisbury, North Carolina)
- Coca-Cola (Atlanta, Georgia)
- Dr Pepper (Waco, Texas)
- Jumbo Orange (Chattanooga, Tennessee)
- Mountain Dew (East Knoxville, Tennesse)
- Nehi Grape and Orange (Columbus, Georgia)
- Pepsi (New Bern, North Carolina)
- RC Cola (Columbus, Georgia)
- Sprite (Atlanta, Georgia)

GRITS PEARL OF WISDOM #15:

If you're going to flavor a Southern tea, the only options are mint and lemon. Anything else would simply be uncivilized.

A Grits Guide to a Well-Stocked Bar

- Stick with the basics: whiskey, scotch, gin, vodka, tequila, rum, vermouth (for cocktails), wine, and beer. A word to the wise: true Grits won't be caught dead with Malibu Rum.

- Keep the mixers straightforward, clear (literally), and easy to use—carbonated water, tonic water, lemon-lime carbonated beverage, and ginger ale. If you're going to drink Coke, drink it straight.

- Have the necessary extras: maraschino cherries, olives, lime and lemon wedges.

- Don't skimp on the ice—allow a pound per person and you'll never go wrong.

- Twenty bar glasses should do—ten 12-ounce all-purpose glasses and ten stemmed wineglasses; if you need more, you might want to reconsider your guest list.

- Don't forget: bottle opener, corkscrew, cocktail napkins, small towel for slops.

- Provide a variety of nonalcoholic beverages for non-drinkers. Iced tea and Coke are always perfect in the South, of course. And for god's sake, keep the bar away from the food table. That is just an accident waiting to happen.

> ## Southern girls know how to loosen a tongue with a Southern touch:
>
> Wild Turkey
> Jack Daniel's
> Jim Beam
> Maker's Mark

Everybody knows that Southerners invented Coca-Cola: it's the pride of Atlanta. They even have a museum there, the World of Coke, which just about sums up the Southern love of this tasty beverage. But did you know we invented all the other cokes mentioned above, and a whole lot more, too? In fact, we can honestly say the South is the place where soda was born—if we ever used the "s" word, that is.

GRITS GLOSSARY

branch water \ 'branch 'wȯtər\ *n : a term coined in the 1800s that refers to pure, clean water drawn from a stream, or "branch"; a bourbon and branch is a bourbon and water, Southern style . ex: "Southern girls know how to make a great bourbon and branch—honey, it's a lot of bourbon and a little splash of branch!"*

And let's not forget that the South is also known for its liquor. From Tennessee and Kentucky bourbon to Southern

Mint Julep

2 cups granulated sugar
2 cups water (branch water is ideal)
Fresh mint
Crushed ice
Kentucky bourbon (2 ounces per serving)

Make a simple syrup by boiling sugar and water together for 5 minutes; cool. Place in a covered container with 6 or 8 bruised mint springs. Refrigerate overnight. Make a julep by filling a julep cup or glass with crushed ice, then adding 1 tablespoon of mint syrup and 2 ounces of bourbon. Stir rapidly with a spoon to frost the outside of the cup. Garnish with a fresh mint spring.

Yield: This makes enough syrup for about 44 mint juleps.

Comfort to the famous moonshining stills on Rocky Top, alcohol has been an important part of our heritage. In fact, some of our most famous citizens are Jack Daniel and Jim Beam, both from Tennessee. They're known the world over for their style, class, and rich, smooth finish.

1 tsp. powdered sugar

4 mint sprigs

Mint Julep

2 oz. bourbon

garnish

shaved ice

straw

Southern as a Mint Julep

The mint julep is the Southern cocktail. Just the name conjures images of genteel gatherings full of men in white suits and women in large hats speaking in a slow, soothing Southern drawl...

A mint julep is a must at least once a year: at Kentucky Derby time. Whether you're at the track in Louisville, Kentucky, or having a small gathering around your television, you'll want to be sure that your mint julep perfectly captures this most Southern of moments. Easy to make, the right Mint Julep will certainly boost your hostess status in the eyes of your guests.

Alcohol isn't just a pastime—there's nothing nicer than a cool verandah and a glass of wine—it's also a social tool. Don't ever be afraid to take advantage of a tipsy man (or woman) to

Grits know where the largest cocktail party in the world can be found: in the parking lot outside the Georgia-Florida football game, of course.

find out all the latest gossip about Billy and Sue. Just make sure you're not the one with the loose lips. If you're starting to feel a little ditzy, put down that cocktail and pick up a nice tall glass of iced tea, or even a coke. Just don't forget to specify which flavor.

More Minty-Fresh Pointers for the Julep of Your Dreams

- Always use a premium Kentucky bourbon, like Maker's Mark.

- Use crushed or shaved ice and pack it in the glass.

- To bruise mint, place in a cup and gently pass the back of a spoon between the cup and the leaves. You want the mint to release some of its fragrant oils.

- Cut the straw to protrude just above the rim of the cup. You should be able to get a faint whiff of the mint sprigs when you're sipping.

- The syrup will keep, covered, in the refrigerator for several days if necessary. (But what a shame if it is!)

CHAPTER 10

Putting on the Grits:

The Grits Guide
to Entertaining

*"Fiddle-dee-dee. War, war, war. This war talk's
spoiling all the fun at every party this spring.
I get so bored I could scream."*
—Scarlett O'Hara

$\mathcal{E}$NTERTAINING IS A WAY OF LIFE FOR THE Southern girl. We've been doing it for over three hundred years now, and we're not too shy to say we're just about the best in the world at it.

There really doesn't have to be an occasion to entertain in the South. Just about any excuse will do, from the anniversary of your friend's divorce (a "comfort" party) to national flag day (Southern girls are always eager to show the flag the respect it's due).

Parties in the South have always been big affairs. In pre—Civil War days, it was a long way between plantations on

GRITS PEARL OF WISDOM #16:

Grits know the main ingredient when entertaining: guests, guests, guests. You get this down, and you'll be doing all right.

bad roads (or no roads at all), so parties lasted for days on end. The hostess spared no expense, with lavish dances, beautiful dresses, and meals that went on and on, with all the best dishes

Who Needs A Holiday?

*L*ike many people, Grits celebrate every conceivable occasion: weddings, birthdays, funerals, anniversaries, holidays, and sporting events. We just do it with more style, hon. We also have a few occasions that really define us:

- **Church pageants.** The church is the best place to congregate for friends, gossip, and potluck suppers. More deviled eggs, please!

- **Derby Day.** There is nothing as Southern as a white suit and a gorgeous hat.

- **Homecoming.** We tailgate all football season—it's almost a religion—but nothing compares to homecoming. Darling, you better watch that mild-mannered man of yours. You never know what's going to happen when he gets together with his old college buddies.

- **Sorority.** Sorority sisters are for life. It's not unusual to see a sixty-year-old steel magnolia dancing and swapping stories with her eighteen-year-old sisters. As a general rule, anything between sisters is within the Grits code of conduct, so cut loose, girl.

- **Family reunion.** A picnic pavilion, a lake, and we are ready to go.

- **Bar mitzvahs, Cinco de Mayo, Kwanzaa, and Bastille Day.** Variety is the spice of life, honey!

- **Cards.** If sipping wine over a game of bridge isn't a Grits tradition, well then nothing is.

continues . . .

- **First day of summer.** Finally, time to hit the pool!

- **First day of school.** Finally, the kids are out of the house! Time to call the girls for a mother's afternoon out.

- **Christmas.** There is nothing bigger than Christmas. Grits have been known to start planning their Christmas parties in June.

the South had to offer: from whole roast pig to wild game stew. After all, plantation parties were a circuit. You might go to twenty parties a year, but you were only going to *throw* one—so you better make it memorable, darlin'.

Grits work hard to keep this tradition alive. The Junior League and Debutante balls are not just coming out parties for

> *A Southern party should be just like everything else a Southern girl does: big, bold, and bright. Class is important, but understatement is for Yankees.*

our daughters, god bless them, they are the modern version of old Southern plantation balls. The same is true of graduation, important birthdays, yearly seasonal galas, and of course our weddings.

Fancy trimmings at any party should always be real—real flowers, real silver, and real crystal.

Entertaining isn't just about putting on a show, though. There's another tradition in the South that's just as important as plantation parties: the gathering of family and friends. Slaves didn't get much time off in the old days, but they knew

The South's Biggest Balls

Even the Somebodys call you a Somebody if you come out at one of these top debutante events—not that the rest of us are jealous, of course. Darlin', we're too busy being soooo happy for you and your mama.

- *Atlanta:* Harvest Ball, Christmas Ball
- *Charleston:* The St. Cecilia Ball
- *Memphis:* Holiday Ball, The Summer Presentation Ball
- *New Orleans:* Debutante Club Ball, Le Debut des Jeunes Filles de la Nouvelle Orleans
- *Raleigh:* The North Carolina Debutante Ball
- *Richmond:* Bal du Bois
- *Savannah:* The Christmas Cotillion
- *The Redneck Riviera:* the Flora-Bama Lounge Mullet Toss

how to make the most of what leisure time they had. They would congregate around simple but delicious meals and sing, dance, and laugh away their troubles—for a few hours, at least.

The work party is also a strong tradition in the South. It was a hard life as a small farmer, and when it came time to plant or harvest, neighbors often came together. While the men worked the fields, the women would prepare an enormous meal: okra, squash casserole, potatoes, collard greens, and maybe even a chicken or two if times were good. At noon, the

first sitting (called dinner) would begin on a long outdoor table, with men eating and women rushing back and forth with

The Power of Hospitality (and Good Cooking)

BY JACKIE VELICKOVICH,
NORTH CAROLINA GRITS

*A*lthough I was born and raised in Lima, Peru, until the age of fourteen, I'm proud to call myself a Southern girl. After all, my family moved to Atlanta in 1979, and my mother has been raising us Southern ever since. To this day, I'm the only Peruvian I know with a real Southern accent!

This doesn't mean my mama hasn't tried to keep both cultures (Southern and South American) alive within our family. That's why we have continued to eat our traditional Christmas feast on December 24, as is customary in most Latin American countries. The next morning, we wake up to a large brunch of leftover turkey sandwiches and good old Southern cheese grits casserole, which was one of the first recipes my mom adopted as her own upon arriving in Atlanta. It's now one of the mainstays of her entertaining.

In good Southern fashion, whenever I brought a friend over during the holiday season, my mother casually explained the meal ritual, Mass schedule, and other unusual (for a Southerner) events to take place around the house a few days before Christmas. That worked fine until one year my boyfriend (now husband) announced, quite vehemently, that he *hated* grits!

It should be noted that Mitch is a very picky eater,

continues...

who to this day has his children convinced he is allergic to all green vegetables. Still, his hatred of our Southern delicacy was almost too much to bear. After a few minutes of stunned silence, my mother simply assured him that he hadn't had *her* grits, and left it at that.

Christmas morning arrived, and amid the excitement of gift giving and calls to Peru, brunch got served. Mitch immediately loaded his plate up with two delicious turkey sandwiches, panetone, and of course cheese grits casserole. He ate with a flourish, never once hesitating or noticing our worried stares. After his third helping of cheese grits, my mom finally asked: "Son, how did you like my grits?"

Well, the poor guy had forgotten all about his apprehension, and had not even realized he was eating grits. Turns out his only previous exposure to grits had been at a Denny's in Miami! Needless to say, this delicious Southern dish, which he now calls with pride his "Georgia ice cream," is a mainstay in our home, and it's all thanks to some fine manners (and cooking) from my sweet Peruvian-Southern mama.

At a successful party, everyone feels at home. A good hostess gives each of her guests a bit of her time throughout the evening. Warm hospitality: that's what being a Grits is all about.

the food and sun tea. After the meal, the women would take the plates away and cover the food with a tablecloth to keep the flies away. At the end of the day, they'd just take the tablecloth away, and supper was ready to eat! Waste not, want not: that's an idea even modern Grits can learn from.

A true Grits will have at least four parties in her home every year. Your house doesn't have to be big—it can even be a trailor—but when it comes to a big party, the kind where you invite the neighbors and all those people you just met, it must

Setting the Perfect Table

Yeah, sugah, there are rules here, too.

- **Know your occasion.** For formal meals, it's fine linen and heirloom lace. For casual, use homey table runners.
- **Add personal touches.** Like a single flower beside each water glass.
- **Mix china and stemware** of various styles.
- **Never serve guests individually.** Honey, it's a party, you don't want to do all that work. Food should either be buffet style from the kitchen or family style at the table.
- **Add easy garnishes** with contrasting colors to each food item.
- **Use several smaller plates and trays,** rather than a single large one. It's more elegant and highlights each dish. Folks got to recognize all that hard work you put in (even if the food is precooked from the super-market).

Grits Guidelines for Successful Entertaining

From the invitation to the drinks, it's all about being creative and making every guest feel at home. Here's a few secrets of the South:

- **Find your own style.** Don't imitate something you liked at another party, unless it was in another city and no one will ever know!

- **Choose colors according to your theme.** One color is always simple, elegant, and dramatic. Two is even better. Three? Now, honey, that's just too much.

- **Use decor to create conversation pieces.** Make use of family jewels like vases, crystal pitchers, china tea cups, and doilies. Just don't let them get ruined, please.

- **Add subtle surprises.** For instance, you can roll face cloths in napkin rings for an elegant touch in the powder room.

- **Don't skimp on quality.** Food and drink must be the best, no matter the budget. If you can't afford to do it right, don't do it. There's no shame in a drinks-only party.

- **Choose the right lighting.** You're going for mood lighting, not the World's Fair. Keep lights low, so your guests all look their best.

- **Send something home with your guests.** Southerners just love tchotchkes.

- **Have backup plans.** A Grits can never be too prepared!

be decked out from the front door to the washroom. Decorations don't have to be expensive, but they should be noticeable.

GRITS PEARL OF WISDOM #19:

Southern girls know the most important accessory is fragrance. Candles and flowers are always a beautiful combination.

A party is a whole-house affair: the decorations, the food, the drink, the ambience, the music, and the fragrance are all important.

Remember, throwing a party is all about planning ahead.

You must be creative and confident, whether planning a big occasion for months or a chic little gathering in a few

WELL, I DECLARE!:
The tradition of "family style" eating, sitting at a long table and taking your portion from a large communal bowl, started at the first working-class Southern get-togethers.

hours. Have a theme, whether it's seasonal, topical, or just a color scheme. Match all your decorations, food, and favors to that scheme. Make sure your invitations, whether written or

Grits Guide to Being the Perfect House Guest

- Be prompt arriving and leaving.
- If staying overnight, be neat. Always make the bed the next morning.
- Ask permission to use the phone
- Respect children and pets—even annoying ones!
- Offer any needed help. It's worth washing a pile of dishes for a great party and the company of friends.
- If coming just to a party, write a thank-you note the next day. If staying overnight, bring a gift or, afterward, send a gift of gratitude.

My Grandmother's House

BY LUCY RINGLEY, TENNESSEE GRITS

*M*y grandparents lived in a rural county in south Alabama, three and a half miles from the nearest neighbor. Like everyone else in the area, life was tough for them during the Depression, and money was very tight. But no matter who stopped by—a musician, a traveler, or a friend—they were always invited for dinner (twelve o'clock meal). Since my grandfather farmed, we always had good food... lots of it. The table would be loaded with bowls of vegetables and platters of fried chicken or beef.

The table was never considered "set" without my grandmother's white tablecloth—starched and ironed, of course. My grandmother presided over this white damask-covered table with all the grace and charm that would be afforded visiting royalty. No matter who the company was they were welcomed graciously. Now that's a woman who knew how to entertain.

A Southern girl knows her outfit is the centerpiece of her party's decor.

verbal, fit the theme *and* inform your guests about the type of party you're throwing. This is your first impression, so make it a good one.

GRITS PEARL OF WISDOM #20:

Preparing for a Southern guest is a labor of love, but remember: after three days, fish and guests start to get unpleasant. After that it's okay to drop-kick that straggler like an old piece of cod, especially if he's your brother-in-law.

Throwing a party is about setting the tone. Start with the number of guests and plan for the crowd. Proper placement of food and beverage tables will control traffic, allowing for relaxed entertaining when the stampede of pearls and patent leather pocketbooks arrives. Just remember to have all your food prepared ahead of time. You do not want to be in the kitchen when the drinks start being poured. It's your party, sugar, and you are there to enjoy it.

Down South there are too many occasions, and too many fine foods, to count. You've got to have your own style, darlin',

Southern girls have more fun . . .
than should be allowed!

or you'll never be a true Grits. Still, there are a few sample menus that should be in any Southern Girl's repertoire—if anybody asks you where you learned them, why you just say they've been in your mama's family for *years.*

Backyard Barbeque
Guacamole with blue corn chips
Texas caviar
Grilled brisket
Chili
Hot potato salad with bacon
Jalapeño cornbread
Fried pies

Low Country Boil
Grits
Assorted vegetables and casseroles
Salmon or crab croquettes
Vinegar pie
Homemade biscuits

Tailgating
It shouldn't be fancy.
Just pick up some fried chicken and coleslaw,
bring along some cookies, and ice down some
cokes, lemonade, and lots of beer.

Family Reunion
Everyone brings their favorite dish.

CHAPTER 11

Let Them Eat Cake:

The Grits Guide
to Weddings

*"I wanted to tie in the Southern things that were special
to me. I wanted the Spanish moss, the moonlight, the
magnolias, the dripping heat of the South, and all of
the traditions and customs that I've grown up with."*
—Kathy Stull, South Carolina Grits

A WEDDING IS JUST ABOUT THE MOST natural thing to a Grits. It combines all our special skills: dressing up, planning, entertaining, and being the center of attention. From childhood, a Grits is trained for her wedding. It's our moment, after all. Oh sure, there's a man there, a wonderful man you're going to spend the rest of your life with (hopefully). We talked about him in an earlier chapter. Right now, let's talk about that other aspect of your wedding: style.

Your wedding says a lot about who you are. Don't rush your decisions. Attend all weddings you're invited to, even if you don't like or know the bride. Await Sunday's paper and read the nuptials. It's a learning curve, darlin', so don't be afraid to study.

In the South, a wedding has always been a way (or excuse)

You want to pull off the perfect wedding? Hire a Grits as your wedding planner!

to gather together friends and family. Whether a lavish wedding on a plantation or a quiet meeting in a cotton field, we tend to make our nuptials a public spectacle . . . and celebration. Grits thrive on giving their sisters, friends, and family the royal treatment, and we've learned that it doesn't take a lot of money to have an exquisite wedding.

WELL, I DECLARE!:

An informal poll puts the average number of bridesmaid dresses in a Southern girl's closet at a whopping *nine*!

Over the years, the nature of weddings has changed. It's now perfectly acceptable for Grits not to get married in the

Tips for Wedding Planning

- Stay calm.
- Make lists.
- Be patient.
- Ask your friends for assistance—they'll be happy to help!
- Choose colors that are appropriate to the season.
- Include the new in-laws (especially your mother-in-law).
- Thank your daddy.

A Real
Southern Wedding

BY JUDY BUTLER,
GEORGIA GRITS

I got married right out of high school in 1965. I was eighteen; my husband-to-be was nineteen. The marriage took place at Brookhaven Methodist Church in Atlanta because my mother's house was right next door. In fact, it was right in the middle of the church parking lot, surrounded by concrete on all four sides!

I can't say it was a traditional Southern wedding. We only had about thirty guests, and my husband and I each had only one attendant. I wore a pink suit—probably the prettiest suit I've ever owned in my life. After the wedding, we went to my mother's house next door for the reception. We served cupcakes and punch.

I have a pet phrase: "You only get one wedding in life: your daughter's." If that's true, I've actually had *two* weddings. Both my daughters were married in big traditional Southern weddings, complete with receptions at the country club.

The truth is, though, that as much as I loved my daughters' weddings (and husbands, bless their hearts), I wouldn't trade my little wedding for anything in the world. We might have been poor back then, but we had the kind of love many couples only dream of.

> *Southern girls know the ingredients of the perfect Southern wedding . . .*
>
> Roses
> Candlelight
> Fifteen bridesmaids
> Reception at the country club

evening in a church. In fact, there are advantages to going another way.

Remember, the wedding is your decision. It's your party, and it's your day. Whatever you decide—small chapel, home,

GRITS PEARL OF WISDOM #21:

Some folks will tell you that if you've had any fun at all before the wedding night, a white dress is not permissible. Excuse me— Grits know that tomorrow is another day! We can wear whatever color we choose. Isn't that right, Scarlett?

garden, pool, or even at sea—is what's best for you. Don't ever second-guess yourself! However, if you want a traditional Grits wedding, some would say the best wedding of them all, there are a few rules you need to follow.

Perks of a Daytime Wedding	Perks of an Evening Wedding	Perks of Eloping
☀ Casual, relaxed, and comfortable atmosphere	☽ More formal	♥ More money for the rock and the honeymoon!
☀ The expense and responsibility of alcohol is unnecessary	☽ More romantic	♥ You don't have to worry about how cousin Edna will look in the bridesmaid's dress
☀ Refreshments can be limited to dessert and a few snacks	☽ A sit-down dinner is a wonderful way to enjoy family and friends	♥ You still get gifts
☀ You can get away, far away, by nightfall	☽ Easier to spend more of Daddy's money (especially effective for annoying a new, young stepmother)	♥ Fewer headaches, more backaches
☀ No lodging is necessary for friends and family who live within driving distance	☽ More of the wondrous pageantry that Southern girls love so much	♥ Your new mother-in-law can't do anything about it until it's too late

• **The announcement.** The first order of business is to let the world know about your nuptials. Unfortunately, in many newspapers today you have to choose between an engagement announcement and a wedding photo. This verges on the criminal, if you ask us. It's a tough choice, but we say go with a wedding picture. After all, with the post-ceremony announcement you avoid alerting those pesky third cousins you'd rather not invite until the party is over.

• **The wedding planner.** Southern girls have been taught to be realistic about most everything they do! We've been trained to know: when in doubt, ask for help. These days, most

Julia Roberts's Wedding

"**S**he tossed aside the typical wedding plan—even the expected A-list guest list. But free spirit Julia Roberts surprised the world on July 4th with a bang bigger than any fireworks: an intimate, romantic, under-the-stars swap of 'I do's' with cameraman Danny Moder."

—*Us* magazine, July 22, 2002

One of the most famous women in the world pulls off a most private affair. Of course she's a Southern girl!

Southern girls are in the midst of busy careers and do not have the time to plan and execute their weddings. We strongly suggest a wedding consultant, coordinator, or a very organized friend. A wedding consultant must think and anticipate. She must be able to fully develop your perfect picture in her mind. She must have style, elegance, and class. She must be a mediator, and a problem solver.

• **The all-important dress.** After you decide the type of wedding and the location, it's time to get down to the decision we've all been waiting for—the dress. We don't need to tell you that you ought to choose a sensational wedding dress. But what does that mean? It's not the fanciest, the one with the most bells and whistles. It's not even the most expensive—sugah, true Grits know how to get *anything* on sale. No, what we mean is finding the dress that makes you feel like the princess you are! It should be appropriate for your shape, relatively comfortable, and something that won't make you cringe when you look back at your wedding pictures in the years to come.

Bridesmaid's Dress Revisited

You may not wear it more than once, but no need to let it collect dust in your closet when you can put it to good use as

- Halloween costume
- A daughter's prom dress
- Placemats or pillows
- Giftwrap (bows especially)
- Christmas tree skirt

Poolside Wedding, Southern Style

*M*y last wedding—hopefully not my *last*, darlin'!—was probably more fun to plan and execute than any of the other three I've had so far. As a mother, teacher, coach, and new business owner, the last luxury I had was time. But since I thought I'd finally met the love of my life (I've since learned we have lots of loves in our lives) I knew I wanted something special and different.

I relied on my friends—Jennifer, Sandy, and the two Paulas—to pitch in and help. Since we all taught school together, it was a snap to plan. In fact, our preparations took all of ten minutes and resulted in the most original wedding arrangement I've ever encountered.

We decided on an afternoon wedding at Jennifer's pool, which was only three blocks from our school. The sweet ladies in our cafeteria made the wedding cake and one of our substitute teachers—the retired Judge Nice, if you can imagine—agreed to marry us.

I wore a simple white (of course) dress and went barefoot. On the day of the wedding, my friends scheduled for their classes to be covered, picked up the cake in the cafeteria, and brought champagne, flowers, good ole Judge Nice (bless his heart), and a camera.

Everything went off without a hitch. After all the toasts were made and the cake was eaten, my friends went

continues...

back to school to finish their classes and my new husband and I left for a short honeymoon.

Even though the marriage is over, my friends and I still talk about the poolside wedding we had so much fun cobbling together. Who knows? Maybe my next business venture will be Grits Weddings, Inc.!

—Deborah Ford

• **Location, location, location.** A traditional Southern wedding takes place in a church—usually Baptist or Methodist, but any denomination will do. Less traditional, but no less Southern, are weddings set in synagogues and other houses of worship, at the country club or under a tent in the backyard.

GRITS PEARL OF WISDOM #22:

Please, girls, remember that wedding pictures and videos live on forevah in Southern libraries. Wear something classy and don't do anything you wouldn't want your mama to hear about.

• **Who's coming to dinner?** Guest lists range in size, but a good traditional wedding has no fewer than one hundred guests . . . more if Daddy's paying. Don't fret if your mother invites a hundred of her closest friends; she's just bragging on you,

What to Take to Your Ceremony

- ✓ Dress
- ✓ Shoes
- ✓ Slip
- ✓ Hosiery
- ✓ Veil
- ✓ Gloves
- ✓ Jewelry
- ✓ Brush
- ✓ Hairspray
- ✓ Lipstick
- ✓ Chalk (in case you get something on your dress)
- ✓ Mirror
- ✓ Tissues
- ✓ Safety pins
- ✓ Lots of prayers

darlin', and most of those women aren't going to show up anyway. The upside is that if they're Grits, they'll all send presents.

• **Flower power.** If flowers are important to Southern entertaining, they are a *must* at Southern weddings. You can never have too many flowers, especially lilies and roses. Try to incorporate some local color: magnolias, dogwoods, camellias, and Spanish moss always offer a nice touch, even if it's just at the reception.

• **The bridesmaid question.** Honey, when it comes to bridesmaids, the more the merrier! Blood sisters, sorority sisters, sisters-in-law, and ex-sisters-in-law are all fair game. Not to mention the cousins! Double-digit ranks are not uncommon or uncivilized. Far tackier would be to leave someone out! Once you've got the list drawn up, be sure to treat these ladies right. They're usually paying their own way, after all, so be kind enough to pick a dress whose style and color is such that these lovely ladies can wear it more than once.

• **Walking the aisle.** No matter how many women are up on stage, the bride is always the star attraction. Make sure you've gotten lots of relaxation and a few good nights of sleep. A Grits girl would never be a pasty-faced, puffy-eyed bride. Splurge! Treat yourself to a massage or two. Have your toes, nails, face, and hair done—you're more than worth it. On the big day, be sure to stand up straight, shoulders back and

Diamonds Are Forevah!

*F*or your second (or third) marriage, combine all your diamonds and have a really dynamic piece of jewelry made for yourself. Remember, Grits need never return gifts men give them! (The only exception is if he's given you his mama's ring, and you've had an amicable parting.)

tummy in, with your bottom curled under your hips. And then walk tall, girl—you'll look five pounds thinner.

• **Get ready to party.** The Southern wedding reception is the biggest party of all, of course! The bad news is, this is one party you're probably not going to get to enjoy. Between talking with second cousin Abner and trying to cut the cake, throw the bouquet, and grab a bite to eat (Grits never eat the

"I incorporated special linen pieces that had belonged to all the women in my family back to my grandmother. By saving their pretty and sentimental things and including them in the wedding, I felt like they were part of it."

—*Retta Wolff, Texas Grits*

morning of their weddings!), you'll be lucky to remember to kiss your new husband. Don't worry, just keep the food, drinks, and music coming and everyone will be satisfied—especially your mother. A month later, you'll even have the pictures to prove it.

• **Send 'em home happy.** In the end, it's the small gestures that make Southern weddings distinct. Thoughtful touches, warm hospitality, and graciousness are the keys to any Southern wedding. Your guests are important, so it's only natural to offer a small parting gift as a memento of the occasion. You want them to remember you, dear! Your attendants' gifts should be creative and personal, even monogrammed. One particularly Southern idea is to give delicate silver bells to the Southern belles, to "ring" in your new life! (Note: Mississippi State alumni may substitute cowbells.)

• **The follow-up.** Finally, it's the ultimate creative undertaking to say thank you 250 times and still sound sincere. Nevertheless, a Southern bride knows she must send a note to each and every person who helped make her day more special. Writing a few at a time will allow you to make them heartfelt and sincere. (It will also keep your hand from getting cramped up, since thank-you notes *must* be handwritten.)

GRITS PEARL OF WISDOM #23:

Do we have to say it again?

Thank-you notes.

Thank-you notes.

Thank-you notes.

PART IV

Strick'ly Southern

CHAPTER 12

Grits Just Wanna Have Fun:

The Grits Guide to Southern Humor

"I am not offended by dumb blonde jokes because I know I'm not dumb. . . . I also know I'm not blonde!"
—Dolly Parton, Tennessee Grits

"If you don't make fun of yourself, somebody is going to do it for you."
—Martie Maguire, Texas Grits and member of the Dixie Chicks

𝒯HERE ARE SOME THINGS IN THIS WORLD that are strictly Southern. You just have to spend some time below the Mason-Dixon line to understand them. You may think you've got football, religion, and humor up North—well, maybe not humor, since we've never known a funny Yankee, including that Seinfeld—but you haven't seen nothing until you've been down South. Really, it's a whole 'nother world down here, and that's what we're here to explain.

Down South, humor is one of our strongest traditions. We love to make fun of outsiders—revenuers, carpetbaggers, or run-of-the-mill Yankees—but most of our humor is centered

"Do Southerners laugh at different things than Northerners do? Yes, I say—Northerners."

Roy Blount, Jr.,
Roy Blount's Book of Southern Humor

Proper Ways to Laugh, Southern Style

- Hold your hand straight over your mouth. Act like you're going to whisper to someone next to you.
- Make eye contact and let the joker know you appreciate the humor.
- Don't be afraid to laugh out loud, but if you can't control yourself after a minute, leave the room!
- Don't ever, ever spit anything out of your mouth. Choke down that white wine and show a little self-control.
- Girl, don't you suck your teeth or roll your eyes at me!

around our very own Southern culture. From overzealous cheerleaders to shirtless rednecks, there's a lot to laugh about down in Dixie, and there is always someone ready to tell tales on a neighbor. All in the name of fun, of course. All in the name of fun.

Southerners know laughter is not just about humor and jokes; it's about relationships. Humor is our way of getting through the rough patches, whether personal, professional, or agricultural. Our humor deals with race, gender, sexual identity, class, occupations, politics, home, neighborhoods, education, and especially family. We know our limits, but we don't consider any group sacred! So don't get offended, now. If we tell a joke on you, that just means you're part of the family.

Southern Humor Hit List

*H*ere are just a few topics to get you started:

- *Yankees.* We know 'em when we see 'em, and so do you.

- *White trash.* It's the way you act, not your socioeconomic standing.

- *Rednecks.* No shirt, no shoes, no service, but plenty of bawdy humor.

- *Sports teams.* It doesn't matter if you haven't played in a decade, we're still mad about that game from 1962. Note: this is the only category of Southern humor truly born of hate.

- *Fans of sports teams.* They bring it on themselves with their shakin', screamin', game-goin' ways.

- *Cheerleaders.* Nothin' but beauty queen wanna-bes.

- *Garden club ladies.* So prim, but so dirty!

- *Marriage.* You better laugh, or the stress will have you pushing up daisies with the garden club sooner than you think.

- *Country club ladies.* Life is nothing but tennis, bridge, dining, and whining.

- *Politicians.* Anyone fool enough to run for office deserves what they get.

These days humor really is a laughing matter, but Southern humor hasn't always been—well, humorous. In the 1800s, Northerners began to joke on Southerners as inbred backwoodsmen and uneducated buffoons, and soon we were all at war. After emancipation, Southerners turned this hard edge back on their own culture, using jokes about African-Americans as a flimsy disguise for racism and hatred.

In the days of segregation, African-Americans used humor in a different way: as a form of defiance and pride. And believe us, they had plenty of material. It's not hard to make fun of white Southern crackers.

Traveling minstrel shows, which often entertained whites and blacks on different nights, were the bee's knees between the Civil War and talking movies. The so-called "Chitlin' Circuit," a standard tour of Southern towns, was the Southern Broadway, just with more belly laughs and less nasty critics. Unfortunately, the big act was blackface, and blackface balladeer Al Jolson was the most famous man of his era. We can assure you, though, that Al's no Elvis. When was the last time you saw footage of Al Jolson swinging his hip on the Vegas strip? That's right: never.

GRITS GLOSSARY

chitlins \ 'chit-lənz\ *n* : *why, they're pig intestines, and they're downright tasty (if you don't think about 'em too hard).*

These days, Southern comedy is the height of gentility. We've learned to love our humor like our lifestyle: laid-back.

> ## *Southerners know television that brings a smile and a good laugh...*
>
> - *The Real McCoys*
> - *The Dukes of Hazzard*
> - *Hee Haw*
> - *The Andy Griffith Show*
> - *The Beverly Hillbillies*
> - The weekly reruns of *My Cousin Vinny* on TBS

Southerners don't go in for cursin', kickin', or callin' Mama names. We love to make fun of ourselves, honey, but it's only play. We save the vitriol for outsiders, husbands, and of course, the sports team the next state over.

Today, Southerners have a wealth of comedy tradition to look back on. Mark Twain may have been from Missouri, but he had the humor of the South down to perfection, not to mention the white Southern suit. (Missourians are honorary Southerners, anyway.)

Hee Haw put the humor into country chic. Minnie Pearl is truly the "Queen of Country Comedy," as she was always known, right down to her intentionally bad singing and the trademark price tag on her hat. And there's nothing funnier than beautiful Southern women with blackened teeth and Daisy Dukes telling jokes in a corn patch. You'll never convince us otherwise, so don't even try.

Lewis Grizzard, longtime columnist for the *Atlanta Journal-Constitution*, was the undisputed king of baby-boomer Southern humor and a man a Grits could look up to. Grizzard coined

You Might Be a Yankee if . . .

(with a special thank you to Jeff Foxworthy for the concept)

1. You don't know what a MoonPie is.

2. You've never had grain alcohol.

3. You think Okra is short for Okrahoma.

4. You eat fried chicken with a knife and fork.

5. You've ever been to a zoo that featured a cow or a chicken.

6. You don't see anything wrong with putting a sweater on a dog.

7. Two generations of your family have been kicked out of the same prep school in Connecticut. Hell, you're a Yankee if two generations of your family have even *been* to prep school.

8. You've never planned a vacation around a gun and knife show.

9. You think more money should go to important scientific research at your university than the salary of the head football coach.

10. You don't have doilies, and you certainly don't know how to make one.

11. You get freaked out when people on the street talk to you.

12. None of your fur coats are homemade.

You'll Laugh Till You Fry

Sara Voorhies, wife of famous Southern humor writer Jack Voorhies, likes to joke about one of our favorite Grits topics: cooking. Specifically, really bad cooking. Here's just an appetizer:

"This is my busy-day supper for Jack:
I take everything from the left side of the refrigerator,
combine it with everything from the right side of the
refrigerator, sprinkle Fritos over the top and bake."

"I've been known to serve a seven-course meal when company comes...a six-pack of Dr Pepper and a MoonPie."

"For a meal with an Italian flair, you can fix my recipe
for Veal Trampolini. It will make your guests jump
up and down."

"A lot of my friends like my recipe for Pullet Mazzerati.
It's a chicken that's been run over by an Italian sports car."

"My Uncle Cut likes to give Jack advice. He says when
you're running from the Revenoores, don't try to run with
half a barrel of corn likker, 'cause it'll run you into every
tree in the forest."

classic phrases like "Chili Dawgs Always Bark at Night" and "Don't Bend Over in the Garden, Granny, You Know Them Taters Got Eyes" and took a profoundly hilarious stance toward everything modern, cold (weather-wise), and Yankee. This was a man who truly hated the very idea of skiing. Lewis passed away in 1994, but he left a legacy of humor that still lives on today.

GRITS PEARL OF WISDOM #24:

If you learn to laugh at yourself, you'll never run out of smiles.

Jeff Foxworthy took the concept of redneck humor to new heights with his *You Might Be a Redneck If...* series of books and comedy shows. Brett Butler used her anger at her upbringing to fuel her rise to stardom on a hit television show.

Country Club Humor

Q. What's a country club lady's definition of a faithful husband?
A. His alimony checks arrive on time.

Q. What's a country club wife's idea of natural child-birth?
A. Absolutely no makeup!

Position your satellite dish directly in front of your trailer. The dish costs considerably more than the trailer, after all, and should therefore be displayed.

Plenty of Grits are out there right now trying there hand at professional comedy. Leslie Norris was runner up in both the Miss Georgia and Miss Florida contests, but that hasn't kept her from being Miss-led on her road to the top, as she likes to say. She's still following in the footsteps of Miss Texas Becky Blaney, who became the first female to win the International Magician's Contest in 1975. Arkansas is home to the very funny Etta Mae, a steamroller of Southern sass. She grew up in Bald Knob with nine brothers who called her the Human Sacrifice. Her humor is filled with pearls of Southern wisdom, and she's got the secret weapon of the Southern girl: a cute double name!

GRITS PEARL OF WISDOM #25:

Tornadoes and Southerners going through a divorce have a lot in common. Sooner or later, someone is going to lose a trailer.

Medical School

Here's a classic bit of country humor from the Paw *and* Pearl *radio show.*

Pearl: Paw ...?

Paw: What is it, Pearl?

Pearl: How do you spell Rat?

Paw: Rat?

Pearl: Uh-huh ... rat.

Paw: R-A-T, I reckon.

Pearl: Naw, I mean rat ... like in rat now.

Paw: Well, lemme see ... uh ... R ...

Pearl: I'm rattin' a letter to my boyfriend, Maynard, to tell him to come home from college rat now ...

Paw: How come?

Pearl: Because Maytag's got the warshin' machine he's been wantin' at a sale price.

Paw: I didn't realize you could rat, Pearl.

Pearl: I cain't, Paw.

Paw: I don't reckon it matters much.

Pearl: Naw ... 'cause Maynard don't know much how to read.

Paw: You say Maynard's in college, Pearl?

Pearl: Yes, sir ... he's in medical school.

Paw: What's he a-studyin'?

Pearl: Maynard ain't studyin' nuthin'—they's studyin' him!

As you can see, the real humor of the South comes from ordinary people. It can be heard in the bars, country clubs, and even the bathrooms of every state below the Mason-Dixon line. We hear you can even read it off the walls in men's bathrooms.

GRITS PEARL OF WISDOM #26:

Don't ever make fun of a fellow Grits girl's weight, clothes, or family, even if she makes fun of them first. It's one thing for her to say, "My crazy aunt Eunice's cooking has made me so fat I can't even fit into my clothes." It's another thing entirely for you to agree.

Southerners have a sense of perspective, a way of finding the humor in even the most painful of experiences. We know that life is too short to be unhappy. Even when we're lower than lizard spit (as Florida Grits Sandra Presley often says), we find a smile.

The best way to know Southern humor is to hear it. The best way to hear it is to come on down South. But please don't come empty-handed. Bring a joke; get a joke. You know what I mean, Vern?

Southerners have always known that laughter is good for you. We'd been laughing at ourselves for many years before research proved that laughter reduces stress, decreases pain, increases energy, inspires creativity, and helps relationships grow. These benefits boost the immune system and strengthen our hearts and lungs. No wonder Southerners are the happiest people around!

Funky Southern Festivals

Our humor isn't all in the comedy clubs. Here are some fine Southern festivals sure to put the tick in your trousers—and the tickle in your funny bone.

Woolly Worm Festival, Banner Elk, North Carolina. If the wool is thick, it's going to be a cold winter.

Frog Festival, Rayne, Louisiana. Proud home of the World Champion Frog Jumping Contest.

Sucker Day, Wetumpka, Oklahoma. In 1950, Wetumkans paid for a circus that never showed up. Now, in good Southern fashion, they laugh at being suckered.

The World Grits Festival, St. George, South Carolina, and the **National Grits Festival, Warwick, Georgia.** Like your grits cooked up in an inflatable kiddie pool? Got your sights set on becoming the next Grits Pageant Queen? Got a hankerin' to throw yourself into a pit full of squishy breakfast cereal? If so, these Southern food fests won't disappoint.

Redneck Rules of Etiquette

- To avoid bruising wine as you decant it, make sure to tilt the paper cup.

- Your centerpiece should never be prepared by a taxidermist.

- When dating (outside the family), always offer to bait your lady's hook, especially on the first date.

- Establish with her parents what time she is expected back. Some will say 10:00 P.M.; others might say Monday. If the latter, it is the man's responsibility to get her to school on time.

- When attending the theater, refrain from talking to the characters on the screen. Tests have proven they can't hear you.

- Never take a beer to a job interview.

- Always identify people in your yard before shooting at them.

- Convenient though it may be, it's considered tacky to bring a cooler to church.

- If you have to vacuum the bed, it is time to change the sheets.

- Even if you're certain you're in the will, don't drive a U-haul to the funeral home.

The sound of laughter is contagious. It's a verbal hug, best shared between friends and family. In today's world, with all the pain and frustration we've seen, you've just got to laugh. Nothing else seems to make sense.

Thank the Lord there's so much to laugh at in this world!

A good joke results in . . .

Head bobbing
Finger pointing
Neck swiveling
Hip swinging
Hair tossing

That's why they say humor is almost as good as sex!

CHAPTER 13

Song of the South:

The Grits Guide
to Southern Music

*"If I had to tell somebody who had never been to the
South, who had never heard of soul music, what it was,
I'd just have to tell him that it's music from the heart,
from the pulse, from the innermost feeling. That's my
soul, that's how I sing. And that's the South."*
—Al Green, legendary soul singer
from Memphis, Tennessee

*"You gotta say Darlin' like ya mean it and sing it,
Darlin', from your soul!"*
—Vestal Goodman, Kentucky Grits and queen of
Southern gospel music

$\mathcal{T}$HE SOUTH GIVES RHYTHM TO THIS GREAT country, and we Southerners are born with that rhythm in our souls. It comes from the fields and streams, and from the soft drone of crickets and cicadas on a warm summer night. Music is in our talk, our walk, and even in our work—from the straight lines of the cotton fields to the tapping of a computer terminal.

Southerners love to make music, and we love to sing about the things we know: our towns, hills, rivers, deltas, beaches, lovers, and our Lord. All define the landscapes of our lives, and

If the sweet lilt of a soft Southern accent isn't music to the ears, we just don't know what is. Music isn't just in our blood, it's in our words as well.

all are defining values in our songs. We've been singing for a long time, and we've never been afraid of a new sound, a new instrument, or a new way of stomping our feet. When you think about it, Southerners have been the impetus behind just about every type of popular music America has to offer. Gospel, country, bluegrass, jazz, blues, zydeco, Tex-Mex, and of course rock 'n' roll—they're all products of the South. We're even responsible for recent teen rock phenomenons like Britney Spears and 'N Sync, if you count Orlando, Florida, as part of the South. Which we do, thank you very much.

Grits are mighty proud of our musical heritage, and of the brothers and sisters who have put our lives to song—and put songs in our lives. A brief survey can never do justice to the song of the South, but that's about all we have time for right now. So start swinging those hips and moving to the beat, y'all—the South is where music to the ears becomes food for the soul.

Southern music has always had two branches: so-called

The Award for the "School with the Most Soul" Goes to . . .

The Stamps-Baxter School, held during the summer at the Belmont Campus of the University of Tennessee in Nashville, is the world's premier school for old-fashioned, belt-it-out-for-the-Lord gospel music. Headed by Southern Gospel legend Ben Speer, the king of shape notes (everybody's king of something in the South), the school keeps alive a tradition of Southern music teaching that has been popular since the 1930s.

The Right Place
at the Right Time

Birthplace of country music: Bristol, Tennessee
Birthplace of blues: Memphis, Tennessee
Birthplace of jazz: New Orleans, Louisiana
Nursemaid of the Delta blues: Clarksdale, Mississippi
Hangout of zydeco: Shreveport, Louisiana
High school mentor of Southern soul: Muscle Shoals,
   Alabama
College drinking buddy of alternative rock: Athens, Georgia
The place where country bought a home and settled down:
   Nashville, Tennessee

white music, and so-called black music. Of course, these distinctions are just so much talk. Blacks and whites have shared music together since the Colonial era. Spirituals and gospel, for example, grew out of nineteenth-century camp meetings where blacks and whites mingled freely. That's what makes them so special. Gospel is the Lord's music, sung by and for all his children. And boy, can Southerners sing it.

The black branch of Southern music includes two of the most important musical innovations of the last hundred years, jazz and blues. Both grew out of the Delta region of Mississippi and Louisiana, but that's about where the similarity ends. Jazz is precise, sophisticated music full of sparkling horns, the product of the cosmopolitan city of New Orleans. Blues is a more throaty indigenous music, often played on old guitars and handmade instruments. It's the perfect embodiment of the

GRITS GLOSSARY

shape notes \\'shāp nōts\\ *n* : *the precise scale notes used in classic gospel singing. ex: "The Lord wouldn't stand for just any old notes being sung now, would he? They've got to be* shaped *just right."*

poor Delta towns and shanty honky-tonks, where it was raised to an art form.

Many people believe that the founder of the blues was a young African-American man named Robert Johnson, whose

Southern girls know the South is full of great music created right in our own backyard . . .

Soul
Blues
Country
Bluegrass
Gospel
Jazz
Zydeco
Rock 'n' Roll

A Grits Girl Goes Glam

"People ask us how we can travel and be to-gether virtually twenty-four hours a day. We've never had a problem that way. We're family and best friends ... We're just the way with each other as we are with anyone else."

—Lynne Spears, mother of Britney and a Tennessee Grits

"*I'*m a Louisiana girl," says Britney Spears. That's true (she's from Kentwood), but to many young girls she also epitomizes the American dream—a small-town Southern girl who headed off with her mother to the Big Apple and made it big. Her first album and first single, both titled *... Baby One More Time*, became the first single/album combination to both reach number one in their first week of release. She has gone on to become one of the best-selling female artists in history, and all before the age of twenty!

The South is a central part of understanding Britney Spears. She is a classic Southern image of femininity: sweet, sultry, and a little bit dangerous. Her Southern roots have kept her groomed—she'd never leave home unless her hair was just right, even if there weren't a hundred photographers ready to snap her picture. And, of course,

continues ...

she still travels with her mama and credits her for all those family beauty pointers.

Now, we're not saying Britney is the epitome of Southern etiquette. We would never let our daughters out of the house in some of those skimpy outfits she wears, no matter how old they were or how much money they could make. Dolly Parton may have invented the over-the-top trashy look, but at least she has a sense of humor about it! And we never got so much as a glimpse of Dolly's belly button.

Still, we're awfully proud of Britney Spears, one very successful Grits girl.

talent for playing just about anything he heard got rumors started that he'd sold his soul to the devil in exchange for his way with a guitar. Johnson was just twenty-seven years old when he died in 1938, and even though he was thrown in an

WELL, I DECLARE!:

Tennessee Grits Aretha Franklin was an unwed mother of two children at the age of seventeen. Think that's hard? Country legend Loretta Lynn had *four* children at that age.

unmarked grave (though Mount Zion Baptist Church in Ita Bena, Mississippi, and Payne Chapel in Quitto, Mississippi,

Southerners don't need instruments, they just use what they've got, like ...

Cigar boxes
Tin cans
Washboards
'Shine jugs
Spoons
Hair combs
Wood saws
Knees and feet
Our voices

both claim him), his legend lives on. His modern-day disciples include Eric Clapton, Led Zeppelin, and the Red Hot Chili Peppers, and it's well nigh impossible to count the number of Englishmen who have gone down among the tar-paper shacks of the Delta looking for the ghost of Robert Johnson.

While black music grew out of the lowlands around the Mississippi, white Southern music stuck to the hills. The

GRITS GLOSSARY

blues \ 'blüz\ n : *nothing but a good man singing about hardship, sorrow, and the things he's done wrong—but sake's alive, they make sadness sound so perty!*

Appalachian hills, that is, where poor white folk picked out wild mountain music on banjos made out of old coffee cans and cigar boxes. It was in those mountains and hollers that Jimmie Rodgers and Bill Monroe first gave the world country and bluegrass. Like the blues, it was the sad sound of poverty that gave the music its beauty.

Today country music is some of the most popular in America, with its roots in the clouds and its heart in Nashville, Tennessee, also known as "Music City, U.S.A." Modern country

Southern Born and Bred

It may not be country or rock, but this Southern music has made an impression on millions:

Southern rhythm and blues. As played by John Lee Hooker, Muddy Waters, and Big Joe Turner. In the 1950s, this was rock and roll.

Southern soul. Who could ever forget Ray Charles, Otis Redding, Aretha Franklin, James Brown, and Gladys Knight?

Roots rock. As played by the Allman Brothers and Lynyrd Skynyrd. It's all about getting back to those Southern roots.

Folk rock. Folk started before the dew was on the mountains, but it got new life in the 1980s from bands like Georgia's Indigo Girls. These Grits know what it means to be Southern, female, and proud.

is the combination of Appalachian banjo and the sound of Texas and the Ozark mountains, as played by Bob Wills, Willie Nelson, Johnny Cash, and Waylon Jennings. It's also a reflection of the South today: smooth, cosmopolitan, and honest as the day is long. There may never be another coal miner's daughter like West Virginia's Loretta Lynn, but country music will always be the music of Southern dreams.

White Southern music and black Southern music finally came together in the 1950s at the urging of Sam Phillips of Sun Records. The voice, and the look, that brought the sound to the public was none other than Elvis Presley.

> *"The colored folk been singin' it and playin' it just the way I'm doin' now, man, for more years than I know. Nobody paid it no mind till I goosed it up."*
>
> —*Elvis Presley*

Elvis was just a small-town Southern boy with a love of gospel music, but he had the good fortune to be handsome as a hound dog and smooth as a summer night. He was born and raised in Tupelo, Mississippi, right up the road from Clarksdale, the home of blues legends like Robert Johnson, Muddy Waters, and Howlin' Wolf.

Southern girls know their women who can belt out a country song . . .

Reba
Wynonna
Naomi
Tammy
Dolly
Crystal
Loretta
Faith
LeAnn

And we will *never* forget the immortal Patsy (Cline, that is).

When Elvis first laid his distinctive sound down on vinyl, then got up on stage and gyrated to the beat, it was nothing short of a revolution. That revolution was called rock and roll, and it's a true son of the South, born and bred from our mutual love and respect for one another.

From Bristol, Virginia, where the legendary Carter Family and Jimmie Rodgers were first recorded; to Nashville, where country music has flourished; to Memphis, Tennessee, where the blues took root; to Muscle Shoals, Alabama, where Southern soul peaked; to New Orleans, where jazz was born; to Macon, Georgia, hometown of Otis Redding, Little Richard, and James Brown and the center of 1970s Southern rock—it can never be denied: music is part of our Southern heritage and our unique gift to the world.

G.R.I.T.S

BY CHUCK LEONARD,
BLUE MILLER, AND GREG CROWE

They're the hot in Hot-lanta
The sweet home in Alabama
They're the Miss in Mississippi
The ooh-la-la in Louisiana

Chorus
Girls Raised in the South
They sure make their mamas proud
Every good ol' boy knows what I'm talking about
Girls Raised in the South

If you take a pinch of ornery
Mix in a cup of "drive you crazy"
Then add you some magnolia
You got yourself a Southern lady

Chorus

From the Texas border to the coast of Florida
The Carolina shores to the hills of Tennessee!
Ain't a red-blooded boy who wouldn't agree
Those girls get to them like they get to me.

G-R-I-T-S
Drop dead gorgeous in a cotton dress
I like biscuits and gravy, but what I love best is
G-R-I-T-S

Chorus

Southern music is the outgrowth of the respect, energy, and enthusiasm Southerners have for life. On any given day, the rhythm of the South may be bluesy, jazzy, countrified, spiritual, or rockin'. Over time it is all these things, because as Southerners we are all these things. Music is a religion to us, it's in our heart and it's in our souls. That's why, no matter where or how you live, it's the songs of the South that soothe the heartbeat of America.

WELL, I DECLARE!:

Johnny Cash was banned from the Grand Ole Opry in 1965 for being too wild! Thankfully, he found the Lord soon thereafter and straightened himself up.

Music is inseparable from the South, so of course Grits girls have to have their own song. The lyrics are by Chuck Leonard,

Queens, Kings, and Fathers of the South

- **Dinah Washington,** queen of the blues
- **W. C. Handy,** father of the blues
- **Jimmie Rodgers,** father of country music
- **Hank Williams,** drunken stepfather of country music
- **Sam Phillips,** father of rock and roll
- **Elvis Presley,** simply the King

Blue Miller, and Greg Crowe, who originally recorded it. It's also been on an album by the female country group Mustang Sally. We think it captures Southern women in all their fiery glory.

> *"I've always thought that between Mississippi, Tennessee, and Alabama, you've got American music history in the twentieth century. When you look, it covered all the main roots of rock 'n' roll, blues, rhythm and blues, country music, and gospel. They're all represented there."*
>
> —*Bob Santelli, former director of education for the Rock and Roll Hall of Fame*

CHAPTER 14

Lawd a'Mercy:

The Grits Guide to Religion

"The Bible Belt likes its religion the same as its whiskey—strong, homemade, and none too subtle."
—Anonymous

$\mathcal{I}$F YOU GREW UP IN THE SOUTH, ESPECIALLY in the Bible Belt of the Deep South, you understand how much religion is a part of the fabric of Southern life. We know the power and promise of contagious, outrageous joy in the Lord, and we know that Sunday is a day set aside for dressing up, visiting friends, and dining with the neighbors. Whether it was the Lord or Mama who decreed it that way, we sometimes aren't so sure.

Religious or not, Grits always follow the Ten Commandments: We don't steal, lie, cheat, or sass our parents. We don't worship any graven idols, although some of us have been known to be seduced by the engraving on a dollar bill....

Practically every religion under the sun can be found in our region—Presbyterian, Anglican, Episcopalian, Church of God, Church of Christ, Jewish, Buddhist, Muslim. One in six

Southerners is Roman Catholic, according to the latest statistical information. We welcome all faiths down South: most people embrace the truth that if a particular faith strikes your heart and feels right to your soul, it's a sign to stay put.

For those not brought up in a strong religious atmosphere, organized religion can be difficult. Many people do not agree with all the beliefs of a particular creed. Lord knows many Southerners struggle with the idea of organized religion, but we all know the Golden Rule: Do unto others as you would have them do unto you. That's the foundation of life down here.

Southerners have always been serious about our religion, and we've always had our own way of celebrating our faith. That's why this chapter is strictly Southern. While the rest of the country thinks of Sunday service as a time to meditate and

Good Lawd!

Now, even those of us who've been singing Southern hymns since time began sometimes forget that that classic hymn is *not* called "All Glory, Lawd, and Honor" but "All Glory, *Laud,* and Honor"! But this mix-up is purely Southern, and we'll forgive it. Other expressions you're likely to hear in a Southern church include:

"Lawd, have mercy!"
"Good Lawd!"
"Lawdy, Lawdy, Lawdy!"

reflect, we view church as a time to get out, get dressed up, and get excited for the Lord. The South has always been about fire and brimstone. That's what religion is all about, after all: passion. If others are willing to die for our sins, the least we can do is really belt out a good hymn about that sacrifice.

WELL, I DECLARE!:

In the late 1980s, the Baptist Church put an ad in a major newspaper that showed how many people in Alabama were going to hell. Many people weren't too happy about this, especially when they found out damnation in their county was running near 90 percent.

Our Southern forefathers (and foremothers) were religious as soon as they hit shore, of course, but there wasn't really such a thing as Southern religion until the great revival meetings of the early 1800s. Southerners have always been suckers

Grits know their belts:

Bible Belt
Sun Belt
Corn Belt
Black Belt
Garter Belt
Daddy's Belt

Bible Belt Values

BY DR. MARLENE MINTS REED,

TEXAS GRITS

*O*ne of the great memories of my childhood is hearing the strains of "When the Roll Is Called Up Yonder, I'll Be There" flood the hot, humid Waco air as my family walked from the car over the baked earth toward the tent revival at my small Baptist church. My life as a university professor has become more and more complex, and my lecturing engagements have taken me further than I could have ever imagined I would go. Still, I cherish the memory of sitting together with my family at the Sunday night ser-vice—laying my head in my mother's lap to take a nap, re-plenishing my energy from the blessed weariness of a full day in "The Lord's House."

The edifices of worship may change—a gold-bedecked Russian Orthodox church in Kiev, Ukraine, or the over-whelming beauty of the painting on the ceiling of the Chapel at the Beeson Divinity School at Samford Univer-sity—but the religious education many of us received in the Bible Belt stays with us and encroaches upon our busy days, reminding us of our true values.

for a good show, and these itinerant preachers gave the best show most country folk had ever seen. They were screaming for glory, shouting down the devil, and baptizing right there in

The Call of the Lord

BY SUE BUCHANAN, TENNESSEE GRITS

*M*y young daughter Dana often visited her grandparents in a small Southern town where every day a siren blew to mark the noon hour. It was so loud that it terrified the poor girl and left her screaming. In order to soothe her and help her understand, her preacher grandpa (my daddy) told her the horn was to let the children know it was time to go home for lunch. He even suggested that Dana say the words "Go home and get your lunch" each time the whistle blew, which she would do at the top of her little lungs, albeit with the fear of god written all over her face.

One Sunday, our entire family was packed into the second row of the church, listening to Dad deliver his sermon. He was pretty wound up that day, if I remember correctly. It was breezy and all the church windows were open.

Well, right in the middle of his railing, and before we realized what was happening, darn it if that noon whistle didn't blow. Dana stood up in the pew, turned toward the three hundred people in the congregation, and shouted, "Go home and get your lunch!"

Do I have to tell you what happened? Church was over at that very moment. No benediction and no sevenfold amen! Later my preacher daddy, who had the world's best sense of humor, admitted: "It wouldn't have been so bad if half the congregation hadn't shouted amen!"

the muddy crick. Southerners rushed into those waters, and that's right where we learned the true meaning of the power and the glory.

GRITS GLOSSARY

revival \ri-'vī-vəl\ *n* : *an all-day meeting where a large group of people get together to shout, shake, forget their cares, and get in touch with their roots; a.k.a. the religious equivalent of a football game*

Southerners aren't afraid to admit we've manifested the power of the Lord in just about every way possible. We've danced in hot, stifling country churches until we've passed out. We've shouted ourselves hoarse for the Lord. We've embraced everything from speaking in tongues to putting our hands in cages full of rattlesnakes to test our faith.

For the most part, though, Southern religion is about decorum. We dress up right, we sit in the pews waving our fans just so, we nod when we're supposed to and whisper amen, and we sing just loud enough for the Lord, but not our neighbors, to hear us. And when the service is over, we make sure we say a kind word or two to the minister on the way out the door. The Lord may work in mysterious ways, after all, but that's no excuse not to act like a lady.

From the Islamic Center in Jonesboro, Arkansas, to the Kahal Kadosh Beth Elohim Jewish temple in Charleston, South Carolina, the South boasts congregations of nearly every

> *Southerners are taught to do the right things. We understand that the other path has consequences, so we always remember to . . .*
>
> - Be thankful
> - Respect ourselves and each other
> - Make friends with our neighbors
> - Replenish our hearts with love daily
> - Dress our best for Sunday service

religion you can put your finger on—and even some that you can't. But as all true Grits know, when you're talking about Southern religion, you're still only talking about two things: the Methodists and the Baptists.

Methodists in the South are like Methodists everywhere: they love short sermons, amateur choirs, and potluck dinner on the lawn after the service. If you mix the Sun Belt with the

WELL, I DECLARE!:
According to a recent survey, the Bible is found in 96 percent of households in the South. We're wondering how many of those households ever look inside.

Bible Belt, you get Southern Methodists: they always soak up the rays of the Lord and look on the bright side of life.

Baptists are another story. There is nothing quite as Southern as a Baptist. We've even got our own branch of the faith, called Southern Baptist, apparently to avoid any confusion. Scratch any Southerner and you're going to hear a Baptist story. Scale any Southern family tree, and you'll find Baptists in the branches. Half the people living in the South right now identify themselves as Baptist. Who do you think put on most of those revival meetings, after all?

The Baptists gave the South Billy Graham and Stonewall Jackson. The Methodists gave the South Martin Luther King, Jr. (Not that we're reading anything into that, we're just stating a fact.)

Baptists put the strictly in our strictly Southern religion. There are a lot of different types of Baptists, of course, but the most common kind don't drink, don't smoke, don't curse, and don't dance. Some don't even play pool. Baptists are fire and brimstone. They're serious about their scripture, and they're serious about their souls. That's what they'll tell you if you ask them, anyway. Like most of us, Baptists have an amazing ability to turn the other cheek, especially on their own little missteps. That's just humanity for you, even here in the South.

There's more to Southern religion than church on Sunday, although many people would like to think that's their only

Growing Up in the House of the Lord

BY DR. ROCHELLE BRUNSON, TEXAS GRITS

*W*hen people find out I grew up in a Southern Baptist minister's home, they always ask what it was like to not be able to dance. I can honestly tell them it was fine, because I don't know any different. Besides, I was able to dance! All right, maybe I had to draw the blinds (God would understand, but the neighbors probably wouldn't!) but even in the house of the Lord I was allowed to be myself.

The difference was that my parents taught me from birth to do what God expected of me, not necessarily what they expected. Whenever I was faced with a dilemma, I just stopped and thought, "What would please God in this situation?" Any time I did something I felt was not right, I told my parents. I honestly couldn't sleep at night if I felt I had disappointed them or done something that was not pleasing to God. My husband hopes our children have that guilt complex, but I'm not holding my breath.

I have absolutely no regrets. I cannot even imagine growing up any better than I did. We did not always have all the material things that my friends had, but it didn't really matter because I had something more precious. I had unconditional love from God and my two parents.

obligation. Religion is in the fabric of Southern life, so it's rooted in everything we do. Before meals, we take a moment to pray. When neighbors are sick or grieving, we show them Christian charity. When crimes occur, we can work up an impressive showing of pious community outrage.

GRITS GLOSSARY

dry county \ 'drī 'kaùn-tē\ *n : a region where, by law, the heathens can drink as much as they like, but only out of sight of the pious; a uniquely Southern construct*

The ultimate symbol of our religious devotion isn't our churches, though it's often beside them. In the South, we understand cemeteries as our final reward, and as Grits, we understand the importance of keeping them in shape. We visit the graves of our ancestors often, especially on a Sunday, and pray for their souls. We picnic in Confederate cemeteries, with their weather-worn memorials, and remember the sacrifices and sins of our past. Cemeteries are sacred ground in the South. They are the place where faith, family, history, and community meet. We can't think of a better definition of the true power of Southern religion.

WELL, I DECLARE!:

Jack Daniel's Old No. 7, the South's most famous whiskey, is distilled in a dry county. Isn't that just so Southern—a little bit of piety hides a whole lot of sin.

The fruit of silence is prayer,
The fruit of prayer is faith,
The fruit of faith is love,
And the fruit of love is silence."

—*Mother Teresa*

Maybe not an official Grits,
but we'll claim her anyhow.

Religion is reassurance. It is community. It is the conductor that helps orchestrate our lives. It allows you to discover who you are, why you're here, and what you do best. Webster's Dictionary defines *orchestrate* as "to arrange or combine so as to achieve a maximum effect." Orchestration means harmonious organization. Wouldn't it be nice to know that your life is harmoniously organized ... not just what you do or when you do it, but how, where, and why as well? Discover these answers for

Three Religious Truths

- Jewish folk do not recognize Jesus as the Messiah.
- Protestant folk do not recognize the Pope as the leader of the Christian faith.
- Baptist folk do not recognize each other at Hooters.

yourself and you'll be well on your way to a more meaningful life.

Religion is not meant to punish us: it is meant to set us free from guilt, anxiety, and discord. This is what we teach our children in the South. We accommodate changing times through unchanging principles. We embrace the future, without forgetting the past. In the South, life is like a tree. The branches shel-

GRITS PEARL OF WISDOM #27:

Count your blessings first thing every morning ... then add to them as the day goes along.

ter us from the tragedies and sorrows of life, but ultimately we have to grow. Seeds are placed within us: the seeds of hope, love, and forgiveness.

Hope never dies, always bringing back joy and keeping peace in our hearts. Grits know that religion is life itself—that quiet escape from the daily grind that has the power to set you free. It is the desire and wherewithal to change the world around you. Your denomination doesn't matter. Your faith doesn't matter. It's the love in your heart that counts.

CHAPTER 15

Southern Religion Part II:

The Grits Guide to Sports

*"In the South, football is confused with religion,
chivalry, the Civil War, and women."*
—Diane Roberts, *The Quotable South*

*"It is no doubt a cliché, yet true:
Southern football is a religion."*
—Willie Morris

$\mathcal{S}$OUTHERNERS ARE ALL ABOUT SPORTS, and not just football. We like sports so much, we tend to think of any recreational activity as a sporting event. From grilling out on Saturday afternoon to the bowl games at the end of the college football season, competition is only a part of the package for the Southern girl. We take time to plan down to the smallest detail: scheduling, location, wardrobe, food, the invitation list, and even the decorations! Like a lot of things Grits, it's all in the presentation, darlin'.

It's true that football is a religion in the South, but it's not the only game in town. No, we're not talking about church-

GRITS PEARL OF WISDOM #30:

For Southern girls, a football game is just like church. We get dressed up in our finest outfits (or at least in our team's colors), prepare a big lunch for family and friends (served out the back of an RV), scream like the holy spirit is upon us, and spend several hours praying for a miracle.

going again: we're talking about the other country-fried sporting religion that's as Southern as corn on the cob on a hot summer day: we're talking about *racing*.

Football, schmootball—NASCAR is *the* quintessential Southern sport. It was born right here in the South when moonshiners started tweaking their engines and modifying their "sleds" to outrun the feds. The first official stock car race took place at Daytona Beach. And we do mean literally on the beach. Today, NASCAR is not only the most popular spectator sport in the South, it's the most watched sport in the entire country. About time you Yankees caught on.

On the other side of the Southern sports fence is horseracing, which started when some folks in Kentucky mixed too much money with too much time on their hands. There's a reason they call horseracing the Sport of Kings, and that's because only kings can afford to participate. But watching the horses, now that's the Sport of Grits. We just love those fancy hats, those two-dollar bets, and all those cool mint juleps. And don't worry, there are just as many shirtless drunks at the Kentucky Derby as there are at Talladega. We told you already, fences in the South are for talking over, not keeping neighbors apart.

If there's one thing the South is known for, even proud of, it's our legendary conflicts on the football field—not to mention all those classic confrontations between fans in the stands.

"I've always pictured myself as a clydesdale."

—Sandra Bullock, *Virginia Grits*

We've said it before, but football really is a religion in our neck of the woods. Southern football is much more than a pastime, it's a way of life.

For true blue Grits, football schedules take precedence over weddings, funerals, births, and most every other life event. In fact, no self-respecting Grits girl would ever schedule her wedding during football season, unless it's an off week, of course. In some circles, it's even considered impolite to die within two weeks of the big game.

Grits know that there really are more important Bowls than the finger bowl!

Iron Bowl
Sugar Bowl
Peach Bowl
Orange Bowl
Cotton Bowl

Sideline Story

BY BARBARA DOOLEY, GEORGIA GRITS

*W*hen you have a lot of children, and we had four, you get worn slap out. By the time the last baby arrives, you just let them do just about whatever they want. We had a rule that our first son, Daniel, could not go to the sidelines with his father, who was the head coach at the University of Georgia at the time, until he was ten years old. Our youngest son, Derek, got this chance a lot sooner.

When Derek was five, Georgia played our biggest in-state rival, Georgia Tech, in Atlanta on Thanksgiving night. We spent Thanksgiving without the coach, then drove to Atlanta for the game. When we got to the hotel, Derek immediately asked his father if he could sit on the sidelines. Feeling guilty about Thanksgiving, Vince compromised and told him that if we were beating Tech by a large score at the end of the third quarter he could go down on the sidelines. There were two rules: he could not get near the team, and he could not get near Dad! At family prayers, Derek prayed, "... and Jesus please let us be beating Tech by a big enough score that I can get to the sidelines."

At the end of the third quarter the score was 42–0, and I thought that was a reasonable lead to take him down to the sidelines. By the time we got to the fence, Tech had scored and it was 42–7. By the time I got him over the

continues...

fence, it was 42–14. By the time I got back to my seat, it was 42–21 and Derek Dooley was pulling on his dad's pants leg.

That night in the hotel, we put the children down in their room and turned out the lights. We went to our adjoining room and Vince turned out the light. I knew, womanly instinct, that something major was about to be said. I just lay there as still as I could, waiting. Finally he said, "Barbara, the strangest thing happened tonight on the sideline. Tech had the ball going down the field to score and Derek was pulling on my pants leg. I pushed him away, anything to get him to turn loose of my leg. Finally when Tech scored, I looked down and said, 'Derek, what do you want?' I was ready for anything except for what he said. He looked up at me with his big brown eyes and said, "Daddy, don't worry about a thing. Jesus is just having a little fun."

Southern women, of course, don't play much football themselves. Truth be told, some of us don't know a touchdown from a turnover. But there's just something about the spectacle of Southern football on a Saturday that shines with the glory of the Lord. It's not just that football is the biggest social event of the fall calendar; we truly see the battle of State U. vs. State College as a religious experience.

Game day traditions like tailgating with old friends and sorority sisters are important parts of Southern football. So are seasonal events like homecoming and the bowl game your team better make this year. Each game, each year, has its own unique personality. In fact, you could write a history of the

South just by quoting the weekly T-shirts that are printed to announce the winner immediately after each game.

Don't ever tell a Southern woman that her football traditions aren't important. And never even *imply* within earshot of

a Grits that cheerleading, dance team, and majorettes aren't sports! Tryouts are just as competitive and practices are just as physically rigorous in cheerleading as they are in football or basketball. And unlike football and basketball players, cheerleaders have to look good while performing their amazing athletic feats.

Sports isn't all about watching, now, honey. Southern women are also known for their prowess on the field. Today, more than ever, sports are part of our daily lives. Sports teach

Southern girls know their four seasons . . .

Recruiting
Spring Training
Practice
Football

A Grits-eye Guide to Football: North vs. South

Women's Accessories
North: ChapStick in back pocket and a $20 bill in the front pocket.
South: Louis Vuitton duffel with two lipsticks, waterproof mascara, and a fifth of bourbon; money isn't necessary—that's what dates are for, sugah.

Stadium
North: College football stadiums hold 20,000 people.
South: High school football stadiums hold 20,000 people.

Fathers
North: Expect their daughters to understand Shakespeare.
South: Expect their daughters to understand pass interference.

Homecoming Queen
North: Also a physics major.
South: Also Miss America.

Getting Tickets
North: Five days before the game you walk into the ticket office on campus.
South: Five months before the game you walk into the ticket office on campus and put your name on a waiting list.

Getting to the Stadium
North: You ask, "Where's the stadium?" When you find it, you walk right in.

continues...

South: When you're near it, you'll hear it. On game day it becomes the state's third largest city.

Parking
North: An hour before game time, the university opens the campus for game parking.
South: RVs sporting their school flags begin arriving on Wednesday for the weekend festivities. The really faithful arrive on Tuesday.

Tailgating
North: Raw meat on a grill, beer with lime in it, listening to local radio station with truck tailgate down.
South: Thirty-foot custom pig-shaped smoker fires up at dawn.

Concessions
North: Drinks served in a paper cup, filled to the top with soda.
South: Drinks served in a plastic cup, with the home team's mascot on it, filled less than halfway with soda, to ensure enough room for bourbon.

When National Anthem Is Played
North: Stands are less than half-full, and less than half the people stand up.
South: A hundred thousand fans, all standing, sing along in perfect four-part harmony.

After the Game
North: The stadium is empty way before the game ends.
South: Another rack of ribs on the smoker. While somebody goes to the nearest package store for more bourbon, planning begins for next week's game.

young women about life. They show them the value of hard work, dedication, self-discipline, setting goals, and working

GRITS PEARL OF WISDOM #29:

Cheerleaders may not sweat, but they do a lot of glistening! Just because Grits make everything they do look easy and graceful, it doesn't mean that it is. These days they even show cheerleading competitions on ESPN.

with others. Through sports, women learn how to deal with the highs of winning and the lows of defeat. And you just never know who's going to make a mint as an athlete, do you?

Southern women athletes have a lot of role models, but it hasn't always been easy for these trailblazing women. Althea

Southern women know their athletic role models . . .

Althea Gibson
Wilma Rudolph
Marion Jones
Mia Hamm
Chamique Holdsclaw
Mary Lou Retton

A Southern
Cheerleader Tells All

BY MELANIE COWART COLLIER,
GEORGIA GRITS

*S*ports is a topic of which I have limited knowledge, despite the fact that I was a cheerleader for six years at a small private school in a small Southern town, Southwest Georgia Academy in Damascus, Georgia. That's located forty miles due west of Dothan, Alabama, and forty-five miles due east of Albany (pronounced Awl-beni), Georgia. At SGA, there was absolutely no requirement to have any intellectual knowledge of the game of football in order to cheer. To this day, I can still go to a football game and have a perfectly marvelous time having no idea what is happening on the field.

The primary requirement to be a cheerleader at SGA in 1979 was to have big hair and look cute in a short skirt. It helped if you could kick your legs really high. After that, the key to being an effective cheerleader was to watch the crowd, not the game. When their hands flew up in the air in a parallel position, you yelled "touchdown." I'm not even sure I knew what a touchdown actually looked like until after I graduated.

The final ingredient of cheerleading was being able to hug. If the players lost, they needed a hug to console their spirits. If they won, a hug could be the beginning of a long and meaningful relationship.

Gibson had to overcome great racial prejudice and financial hardship to reach the top of the tennis world. Althea won both Wimbledon and the U.S. Nationals in 1957 and 1958.

Wilma Rudolph, who could barely walk as a child, brought home three Olympic gold medals in the sprints in 1960. The seventeenth child of a poor Tennessee family, she went from an average student at Tennessee State University to being one of the greatest women athletes in history.

Florida Grits Chris Evert exemplified beauty and graciousness on the tennis court, both in victory and defeat. Despite her unfair reputation as "The Ice Queen," Evert melted America's heart by winning at least one of the four major championships for thirteen consecutive years, including six U.S. Opens.

Southern women also know the meaning of team. Our universities have long dominated women's sports like swimming, gymnastics, and tennis. The North Carolina women's soccer team and the Tennessee women's basketball team are two of the most successful sports programs in the history of the NCAA. If these were male teams, they'd be heading the parade as the pride of the South. At least now that there are profes-

---

Basic Rules of Cheerleading

- Smile and look like you're having fun.
- Pay attention to the team, and the crowd.
- Act like you know what is going on, especially when you don't.
- If you make a mistake, toss your hair and smile.

Vonetta's Sweet Home

"*I* lived in a place where historic moments shaped our country, a place that is known for biblical teachings and a place where families from all over the U.S. come to visit because their roots are deeply planted here. I was taught to respect others at an early age. I learned the importance of a strong family bond, and I realized why people sang songs like "Down by the Riverside." You gotta love a place whose past is rich in history, a place that is presently taking bold steps toward building a brighter future for our youth, and a place anyone would love to call home... Sweet Home Alabama!"

—Vonetta Flowers, Alabama Grits

sional women's basketball and soccer leagues, these women can pursue their sports as paying careers. It's our job to go out and support them, like true Sisters of the South.

Vonetta Flowers epitomizes the Grits spirit. A promising sprinter, she went through five surgeries in eight years and still refused to back down from challenges. When she was cut from the United States summer Olympic team, she answered an ad for a bobsledder on the winter Olympic team. She had never competed in bobsled before. In fact, being a true Southern Girl, she had only seen snow a few times in her life. Amazingly, she beat the odds to become the first black female athlete to win a gold medal in any winter Olympics. As Grits, we couldn't be prouder of our Southern sister. Vonetta, you go, girl!

In the end, it's not the stars alone who make sports such a part of our Southern heritage. It is the women at the track and in the gym working every day to improve their health and their fitness. It's the young girls who compete in soccer, softball, and basketball leagues all across the South. It's the mothers who make sure their athletes eat right, dress right, and act right on the field.

Grits love to win, but we understand that it's even more important to play the game right. That's what we call Southern charm.

Kentucky girls are ...
The thoroughbreds of the South

PART V

Southern Family

CHAPTER 16

Who're Your People?

The Grits Guide to Southerners

"I've learned to rely on the strength I inherited from all those who came before me . . . I go forth alone and stand as ten thousand."
—Oprah Winfrey, Mississippi Grits

*T*HERE'S NOTHING AS COZY AS THE MEMORIES of a childhood spent in the South. There were summer nights spent on the front porch making homemade ice cream; afternoons spent by the barbeque; winters spent waiting for the occasional snowfall so we could make snow cream. More afternoons eating barbeque, early mornings out in the woods picking wild plums and blackberries, late nights stargazing out in the field, and did we mention barbeque?

Who could forget making mud pies after a rain? Or sneaking into the neighbor's yard to break open ripened watermelons; making houses from bales of hay; riding our first horse

GRITS GLOSSARY

parch \'pärch\ *n* : *the sitting place on the front of a house, known in Northern states as a* porch. *ex: "If you're feelin' a mite parched while sitting' out there on yer parch, a tall glass of Southern lemonade is jes what you need."*

without a saddle; feeling the warm dust between your toes while walking barefoot on a country road? We'll always cherish those nights we spent listening to crickets from inside a tent made of Grandma's quilts; days catching Junebugs and July flies; afternoons getting up the courage to put our first worm

Life is good in the South, and it's not just the weather. It's the people. Southerners know how to live with an attitude of gratitude. We take things slow, enjoy every day, and make the most of what we have.

on a homemade fish hook. We were once twelve-year-olds learning to drive a stick shift in our neighbor's truck. We felt like we were on top of the world when we got to ride on a trailer load of cotton on its way to the gin. We got to milk cows, churn butter, and gather eggs from the chicken coop. We won blue and green and gold ribbons in the 4-H sewing contest; slept with our sisters when it was too cold to sleep alone; waited anxiously as our mothers wrapped a heated iron with a towel to put at the foot of the bed to keep our feet warm. And of course, we played tennis for hours—then jumped into that deliciously cool swimming pool.

What's the effect of this attitude of gratitude on Southern children? Well, we think it's summed up by this description of Mississippi Grits Sela Ward: "Her niceness is genuine, the product of a small-town Southern upbringing that left her with a lasting appreciation for the generosity of spirits that surrounded

Close as Kudzu

*I*n the South, we have a saying to describe how we feel about those around us: "close as kudzu," which means we're all connected at the roots. Of course, the first reply of some Yankees is: "What's kudzu?" If you're going to be a Grits, sugah, you absolutely have to know the answer to this question.

Kudzu is a beautiful green leafy vine. If you've ever driven through the Deep South, you've seen it growing along the side of the road—and right over everything in its path, from trees and bushes to cars, homes, and utility poles. If you stand still long enough in the South, kudzu will grow right over you. The vines grow as much as a foot a day, and in some places one plant can literally stretch for miles. That's why we say we're close as kudzu down here—we're all part of one culture, and we're all connected in some way.

The thing about kudzu is, it's not even native. It was brought over from Japan for the 1876 Centennial Exposition in Philadelphia. In the 1930s, the government planted it across the South as a means of erosion control. Like many before and since, kudzu fell in love with the South and just decided to stay. And who can really blame it, now?

her as a child. It's not just about disarming smiles and gracious manners, though they're part of her charm. It's more about her openness, her unpretentiousness, and her self-deprecating sense of humor." We couldn't have said it better ourselves.

We aren't slow in the South; we just savor our moments.

Southerners can sit on a porch all afternoon trying to guess the color of the next car that comes around the bend. Every time you guess right, you win. What do you win? Why, nothing but pride and the contentment of spending a beautiful afternoon outside with family and friends. And down here, that's everything.

Porches are an important part of Southern life. They give us a place that's all our own, but exposed to the world. We put

> *"Southerners have a genius for psychological alchemy . . . If something intolerable simply cannot be changed, driven away, or shot, they will not only tolerate it but take pride in it as well."*
> —*Florence King, Mississippi Grits*

GRITS GLOSSARY

hillbilly \ 'hil-,bi-lē\ *n* : *a derogatory term that refers to people living in the next county or town; alternate forms include redneck, cracker, hilljack, swamp rat, hick, and Yankee*

our porches on the front of our houses, not the back, so that anybody can come by for a meet-and-greet and a glass of iced tea. We don't want our privacy, we want the world on our doorstep. That's just the proper way to live, darlin'.

Southerners know the meaning of community. We don't draw a line in the dirt, and we don't fence ourselves in. We use our fences as sharing lines, as places to lean over and say a few words to the neighbor. Whether in the country or the suburbs,

GRITS GLOSSARY

Southern checkers \ 'sə-<u>th</u>ərn 'che-kərs\ *n* : *a game played between two strangers who find out they're both Grits; it always begins with the same question—"Who're your people?"—and then traces the lineage of mothers, grandparents, aunts, uncles, friends, and neighbors to the same conclusion: "Why, we're practically sisters!"*

"It doesn't matter where you go in the South, because the whole South seems to be married to one another."

—*Marlyn Swartz, Texas Grits*

in the South fences bring us together, they don't keep us apart. I hope you can say the same about the fences in your neighborhood.

From cotton fields to country clubs, we are all family in the South. Southerners know where people came from, how they

Grandma's Sunday Dinner

BY ROXIE OLLIE BAKER FIRESTONE, ARKANSAS GRITS

Feeding the hungry, physically and spiritually, was the simple strength of my Southern mother and my mother's mother. Every Sunday after church, folks from our church and other denominations would gather at my old country home in Leslie, Arkansas, for fellowship over a big meal of cornbread, buttermilk biscuits, chicken and dumplings, ham fresh from the smokehouse, and fresh garden vegetables. Of course, desserts—cakes, and apple and peach fried pies—were the crowning touch. The menu might change depending on the season, but the warmth and laughter of good neighbors and friends never did. Even in the midst of twenty or thirty folks, I heard my great-grandmother again and again say to all the children present, "Pass to the left," "Napkin in the lap," and of course, "Excuse me."

Even today, a smile crosses my face when I picture the neighbors, clergy, family, friends, and a few strangers at our bountiful Sunday spread. That meal wasn't about food, it was an act of bonding, healing, and sharing. I have passed down to my children and grandchildren (and I'm proud to admit even some great-grandchildren) this simple celebration of country community. Respect and appreciation for others, after all, is my legacy as a Southern girl.

Southerners may all be similar, but we definitely aren't the same. For all you neophyte Grits, here's a quick guide to what to expect below the Mason-Dixon line:

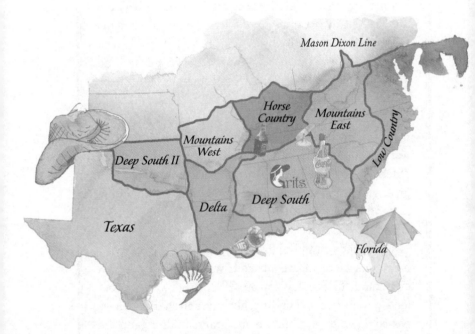

The Mountains—Living isn't easy in the hollers and hilltops of Appalachia and the Ozarks (unless you've retired there), but it's beautiful country. The people have a lot of pride, and make the best down-home music you've ever heard.

Low Country—This is the heart of the plantation belt, where people still talk with a high Southern accent and wear white suits and full dresses, even in the hu-midi-tay.

Florida—Florida has it all, from Orlando and Miami to the Weeki Watchee Mermaids and the Redneck Riviera (otherwise known as the panhandle). And Lord knows all Grits (especially those Florida girls) love to beach, beach, beach.

Horse Country—Living is civilized in horse country, as long as you know one crucial thing: the difference between horse sense and being a horse's behind.

The Deep South—Hot, humid, and flat, this area's been called everything from the Cotton Belt to the Bible Belt to Hell on Earth. Grits know the truth, though: it's paradise. Same holds true for Oklahoma, by the way—a little piece of Deep South in the middle west.

The Delta—Food, music, mosquitoes, and the best party (Mardi Gras) on the face of the planet. What more could you ask for?

Texas—Everything's big in Texas—hair, boobs, attitude and good times. You have to love any state that can take a 1970s anti-litter campaign slogan — "Don't Mess With Texas" — and turn it into the nation's best state motto.

got there, where they lived, where they are buried, and who married whom or shouldn't have or didn't. We eat dinner together with our family and friends, we pray before we eat, we take Sunday drives after church to see our neighbors, we forget to watch our football games because of the great conversation, and we still address our seniors with "yes, sir" and "yes, ma'am."

That doesn't necessarily mean we're all alike. There's nothing Southerners love better than to pick on each other. Virginia makes fun of Tennessee. Tennessee cracks jokes about Alabama. Alabama turns the jokes around on Mississippi. Mississippi picks on Louisiana, and on down the line. But

WELL, I DECLARE!:
In 1807, there were half a million West Africans in the United States. By 1860, the black population was over 4.5 million. Today, one in five Southerners is African-American.

Physically and socially, Florida has its own North and South, but its northern area is strictly Southern and its southern area is definitely Northern.

—Florida: A Guide to the Southernmost State
by the Federal Writers' Project

> ## Southern girls know the sweet smells of summer...
>
> Confederate jasmine
> Sweet wisteria
> Purple lilac
> Suntan lotion

that's just having some fun, now. Southerners will band together in a second against outsiders—at least when it's not football season, that is.

If the South is a family, it has had its share of dysfunction. We know it, and we've paid the price—from having our society torn down by war, to racism as a constant element of our past. The problem started with the plantations, which were families

GRITS GLOSSARY

newcomer \ 'nü-,kə-mər\ *n* : *any neighbor who has lived there less than ten years, unless her mother is from the area, of course*

in the worst possible way. The owner was supposed to be a father to his extended kith and kin, which pretty much included everyone for miles around. But by the 1800s, with some exceptions, plantation owners were exactly the kind of father you don't want to be living with—overbearing, selfish, prone to violence, and totally indifferent to your personal health, wishes, and well-being.

GRITS PEARL OF WISDOM #31:

Grits can admit their mistakes—and we all make some bad ones—but we never accept defeat.

Southerners have learned to thrive in adversity by finding strength in each other. Blacks, especially, learned to be flexible in order to survive. As families were split apart by indifferent owners, the slave community came together to nurture the lost, lonely, and heartbroken. Later, the black community bonded through its churches, schools, and social organizations, with Southern women forming the backbone of its strength. This spirit of community helped black Southerners survive slavery, the Civil War, Jim Crow, segregation, and the Civil Rights struggle with a dignity and character that is a model for persecuted people around the globe.

"All well-raised Southern girls know it's far easier to get forgiveness than permission."
—*Virginia Darmer, Alabama Grits*

Always a Southern Girl

BY BARBARA ARDEN, ALABAMA GRITS

I am a Southern girl who has lived in California for more than three decades. I love it here, but I admit there are many times I still long for those warm Southern evenings. I go home each summer to look for the fireflies, the ones I used to catch and place in a fruit jar and watch in amazement as they continued to show their lights. As I walk through my California garden, I yearn to see just one June bug, the kind that's so big you can tie a string to its leg and watch it race around your head in a circle.

The aging process only magnifies and makes me appreciate the lessons learned in the South during my youth. I have heard the voice of my mother in my head all my life. I feel her strength and I know that my responsibility is to live a full life and contribute to the lives of those around me.

My childhood neighbor, Miss Edna, was my mentor. She lives in me as a constant reminder that long white gloves and a hat in church are the basis of the good life. My memories of Miss Edna remind me that I should always walk straight, set a proper table, and keep my perspective. It is this training that keeps me from joining the "road rage" of the California freeways and the rudeness of a fast-paced lifestyle.

I was a part of the generation of Grits who grew up on the farms, hung out at the grocery stores, and worked our

continues ...

way through college, the first women in our families to get a higher education. In my youth, we were afraid of the H-bomb, tornadoes, and communists. Our protection was the bomb/tornado shelters and church on Wednesday nights and Sundays. These places were a constant symbol of the hope for a better life.

In my present environment, I have lost the sweet tang of my Southern drawl. However, the first step off the plane, the rush of the Southern summer heat, the sheer friendliness of those around me, and "Hey, how y'all doing . . . I am home again!"

Even today, the South is a divided family. We may all mean well now, but it takes a long time to undo the sins of the past. Black and white Southerners are often like two sisters, still fighting over all the cruel things that happened in childhood and adolescence—and still hurting each other with thoughtless acts. Never doubt, though, that we will grow to be the best of friends, because in the end we share the same blood, the same beliefs, and the same heritage. In the end, we're all Grits.

WELL, I DECLARE!:

The air conditioner changed the history of the South because it finally made it bearable to be inside on a summer day. Before that, a shady porch with a nice breeze was the only way to keep cool in the summer heat. On hot nights, Southerners used to sleep on their porches, often more than ten people at a time, which would have been quite a sight.

Southerners have a lot to be proud of. We have survived, and we have overcome. Southern women, especially, have learned to be proud of what they have and patient for what they want—even revenge. That which doesn't kill us makes us stronger, as the old saying goes, and darlin', there is just no way to ever kill the pride and joy of being a Grits.

Wisdom, courage, sacrifice, and determination are the lessons of our history. Southerners know and understand our past as a people, which is why we are all connected, no matter our status in life. We recognize kinship as the golden threads that are woven through our past: the struggles, the pain, and the power of overcoming.

And whether black or white, it is the Southern woman who has held our society together through thick and thin.

"When a New Yorker asked a Savannah society woman what she did, she looked at him, puzzled, 'Why ah live—ah live in Sa-vannah!' she replied with proper hauteur."

—Rosemary Daniell, writer and Georgia Grits

CHAPTER 17

The Ties That Bind (and Sometimes Strangle)

The Grits Guide to Family

*"My family directly and my people
indirectly have given me the kind of strength
that enables me to go anywhere."*
—Maya Angelou, Mississippi Grits

*"No one in the South ever asks if you have crazy people
in your family. They just ask what side they're on."*
—Julia, played by Tennessee Grits Dixie Carter,
on *Designing Women*

$\mathcal{T}$HERE IS NO SUBSTITUTE FOR FAMILY. YOU can't run out on them, and you can't ever lose them. Your family is with you always, and if you let it, your family will always be a source of strength, even if they sometimes seem like a royal pain in the rear.

The Southern family is our strongest weapon. When we've had nothing else in our lives, we've always had family. In the past, the family was the source of our survival. It provided the basics: food, shelter, warmth, the Bible, clean clothes, and a switch in every corner. Maybe that's why after the Civil War there was such an intense effort by freed slaves to reunite with lost children, spouses, and relatives. Family gives you a place where you belong.

GRITS PEARL OF WISDOM #32:

The cheapest way to have your family tree traced is to run for public office.

Black and white, Grits are committed to the idea of family. Our ancestors adapted, adjusted, stretched, adopted, did without and did whatever was necessary to maintain families in spite of all obstacles. It just wouldn't be right for us not to treasure this valuable heritage. Where we love is home. Our feet may leave, but our heartfelt memories go on forever.

Many people joke that a Southern family tree is like a

Lessons in Character

BY MELINDA LEWIS, ALABAMA GRITS

As much as I hate to admit it now (okay, I don't hate it that much), I flunked out of the University of Alabama after my freshman year with a 0.0 GPA. It had been a fun year, needless to say, and I came back home ready to enjoy a summer lounging around the pool. So you can imagine my surprise when, at 7 A.M. the first morning, my mother (country club matron that she was) walked into my bedroom, flipped on the light, and said I had thirty minutes to get dressed and get in the car. I was *not* to return home without a job.

I spent the day searching for a job, not having a clue where or how to look for one, and by 4 P.M. I was exhausted, worried, and jobless. About halfway home, ready to admit defeat, I noticed I was behind a van full of children. I followed the van to a day care, thinking about the number of children in the van and praying the day care needed help.

I got the first job of my life that afternoon, and to this day I still thank my mother for it. That summer changed my life!

Southern pine, tall and straight without many branches. Nothing could be farther from the truth. A Southern family is a magnolia, broad-limbed, leafy, and wide enough to encompass everyone: parents, grandparents, siblings, aunts, uncles, cousins (to at least the fifth remove), and even close friends and neighbors who have become honorary family members.

It's inclusiveness that makes the Southern family so special. Southern children often spend summers with other relatives. They call cherished family friends "uncle" or "aunt." In broken homes, grandparents are often the ones who offer love, support, time, and positive reinforcement, providing a solid foundation for a positive life. All these people, by their example, teach us the power of love and loyalty.

The center of the Southern family, though, is Mama and Daddy. Mothers in particular are a source of pride, inspiration,

WELL, I DECLARE!:

You may be asking yourself, now what are mothers worth? $641,000 annually, according to a study conducted by Edelmon Financial Services. That number was derived from the average salaries of the seventeen occupations a multitasking mother performs during the course of a year, including chef, childcare specialist, psychologist, housekeeper, management analyst, and animal caretaker.

embarrassment, and dread; after all, we're going to end up *being* our mamas someday. When that day comes, we'll know how much our mothers sacrificed, and how much their love meant.

My Daddy and My Car

BY MARILYN AKERS,

GEORGIA GRITS

*A*t fifteen, I came home from school one afternoon to find a faded red car with a white hardtop and a damaged front fender parked in the driveway. Since my daddy often worked on cars, both for himself and others, I noticed it only in passing. That is until my daddy explained that it was a 1971 Mercury Comet... and it was mine!

Trouble was, it had a blown engine, and it was my job to overhaul it. So after school and on weekends I washed car parts, rode to the junk yard for replacement parts (and foot-long hot dogs from the Dairy Queen), handed my dad all sorts of tools, fixed coffee with cream and sugar, and occasionally got to do a "real" job under the hood. I remember being so excited when he asked me to get on the creeper and roll *under* the car (the children were never allowed *under* the car!) to tighten a fender bolt.

Another day, I helped him connect the spark-plug wires to the distributor cap. I asked him why this particular job was so important for him to show me. He replied, "So if you're ever out with a boy and the car breaks down, you'll know what to look for." He meant intentional removal of the wires, and it didn't occur to me until many years later to ask if that advice was from personal experience!

When the engine work was done, we took it to Earl

continues...

Scheib for one of his infamous $99 paint jobs. I was so proud of that car and the work done side by side with my dad. We sold it less than a year later, after I stuck my foot through a rusted hole in the floorboard.

I lost my dad in 2001 following a sixteen-year battle with Alzheimer's Disease. But the bond formed between a teenage daughter and her father, and the lessons I learned from him, will be with me for a lifetime.

It's just a shame it sometimes takes having daughters of our own to really appreciate our mothers.

A mother is special, but the real love of a Southern girl is her daddy. Southern men tend to be the quiet type. They don't talk much, and often they don't seem to understand much, either. A Southern man can sometimes seem more interested in football, carpentry, or cars than his daughter's dating problems.

GRITS PEARL OF WISDOM #33:

You don't have to be born with a silver spoon in your mouth to live a rich life. Stainless steel is more practical, anyhow!

The South *is* the Bible Belt, and our daddies tend to put that belt to good use, too. The idea that to spare the rod is to spoil the child still has deep roots in Southern culture. But deep down, we know that Daddy means love.

Southern girls have been known to call their mamas every day for their entire lives—sometimes more than once. That's almost never true of their daddies. Southern girls put their daddies on a pedestal. They don't want to talk to them, they want to look up to them. After all, Daddy is the ideal man to marry; the perfect fishing partner; the right shoulder to cry on. Usually, it's only later we find out that Daddy was the perfect man to talk to as well.

Southern women pass on child-rearing tips by setting a good example. Over the years, Grits have learned . . .

Never To...	*To Always...*
. . . make a promise you can't keep	. . . be there
. . . cook a meal for your kids that you wouldn't eat yourself	. . . listen more than you talk
. . . smoke or curse in front of children	. . . admit your mistakes— and especially those of your husband
. . . blame a child before yourself	. . . give children space to grow
. . . lose your temper, even when you have a good reason	. . . remember there is no perfect child
	. . . remember there is no perfect parent

Grits <u>always</u> call their parents by their real names—Mama and Daddy.

It used to be that families were always together. These days, Grits are as likely to live in New York City or on the West Coast as they are to live in Mama's hometown. That's why one Southern tradition has become more important than ever: the family reunion. Reunions used to occur every year and draw hundreds of people. You knew everybody and all their secrets, and it was little more than a party. Now reunions may be the

There's One in Every Family

BY GINGER MERRILL, FLORIDA GRITS

When I was a little girl, my cousin Don was the sheriff of our county. He was kind of like a handsome Barney on *The Andy Griffith Show*, and he was always trying to impress us with his job status. One day, while all the cousins were visiting, he stopped by Grandma's farm in his police car. He was showing off his handcuffs and attached them to his wrist and then to the side mirror of his car. About a minute later he realized he didn't have the keys to the handcuffs. We had to call the sheriff's office and get one of the deputies to come out and release him!

Our People

Great Grandpappy

Grandpappy's Spinster Sister

Aunt's Stepniece-in-law

Merl

Uncle Bud, the neighbor

Aunt Flo

Second cousin three times removed

Grandmama

Grandaddy

Spoiled cousin

Drunk uncle

Sweet aunt

Whiny sister

Big brother

Little sister

Mama

Daddy

Stepdaddy

SOUTHERN FAMILY TREE

only time you get to see your extended family—or even that sibling you haven't spoken to since she stole Mama's iron skillet. These days, family reunions are so important they should be on every Grits social calendar. If your family doesn't have a tradition of reunions, honey, it just might be your job to start one.

Labor Day has long been considered *the* family reunion weekend. The summer heat is beginning to ebb, and you can feel autumn in the air. The ingredients are simple: an outdoor grill with hamburgers, hot dogs, and ribs; seats for groups to sit

It's in the Genes . . .

We share 50 percent of our parents' genes; 50 percent of our brother's genes; 25 percent of our aunt's and uncle's genes; 25 percent of our grandparent's genes. Of course, we share 100 percent of our sister's jeans—and the rest of her wardrobe, too!

Starting a Gingerbread House Tradition

*F*amilies are about traditions. If your family doesn't have any, of if you don't like the ones you do have, it's time to take matters into your own hands. There are thousands of traditions you can start: bake or decorate cookies for the holidays; make jam in the summer or can vegetables in the fall; plant a tree in memory of each family member; or plan an annual family reunion. Since we don't have room to explain them all, we've chosen one tradition that is simple, easy, fun, and a classic of a Southern Christmas: the graham cracker "gingerbread house." After all, this wouldn't be a real Southern guide if we didn't mention those two Southern delights—graham crackers and Nilla Wafers.

For this project, you will need: seven graham crackers; frosting that hardens when it dries; Nilla Wafers; plenty of candy and other treats. You will also need a pastry bag for squeezing the frosting. If you don't have a pastry bag, you can improvise by poking a small hole in the bottom corner of a Ziploc sandwich bag.

Construction:

1. Place a graham cracker flat on the table and squeeze frosting along all four edges.

2. Stand a graham cracker along each edge (use

continues ...

halves on the ends). Put frosting in the corners and hold crackers until the frosting begins to dry. Let stand for about fifteen minutes, or until frosting hardens.

3. Squeeze frosting along the top edge of the two long standing graham crackers. Place the remaining two graham crackers on top, forming an inverted V. Squeeze frosting along the top of the inverted V. If you wish to form eaves by allowing the graham crackers to hang over the outer walls, you will need to hold them in place until the frosting dries.

4. Now comes the fun part: decorating your house. Using the rest of your frosting as a base, place your goodies on the house to form shingles, windows, doors, and other interesting designs.

Note: this is a basic recipe. Larger and more complex houses can be made using more graham crackers. No matter what the size, graham cracker gingerbread houses are edible. However, they taste best when eaten within a day or two of construction!

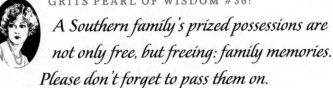

GRITS PEARL OF WISDOM #36:

A Southern family's prized possessions are not only free, but freeing: family memories. Please don't forget to pass them on.

around and tell tales and yarns on one another. Any old park will do, as long as there's a horseshoe pitch and a volleyball net. Throw in a lake, a boat, and a field for softball, and darlin', you've got all the ingredients for a classic Southern family reunion. Just make sure someone remembers to bring deviled eggs, a camera, and plenty of ice-cold beer.

Family closeness does not come easy; it is a gift we create through sacrifice and hard work. It is the result of years of trust and dependence on one another. Once established, it offers the comfort and joy of being together, and being ourselves. We become responsible for nurturing each other's growth, forging ties that bind us together, as family.

"I'm a godmother, that's a great thing to be, a godmother. She calls me god for short, that's cute, I taught her that."

—*Ellen DeGeneres, Louisiana Grits*

CHAPTER 18

Making Us Proud:

The Grits Guide to Successful Southern Women

*"You've got to continue to grow, or you're just like last
night's cornbread—stale and dry."*
—Loretta Lynn, Kentucky Grits

*"Don't tell me I can't do something,
'cause I'll show you I can."*
—Tammy Wynette, legendary country singer
and Alabama Grits

*A*FTER OUR OWN KIN AND OUR BLOOD, there's nothing more important to us than the family of Southern women. That's what being a Grits is all about, darlin': success, pride, and love of life.

We should never doubt that a small group of thoughtful, committed citizens can change the world. Women have always understood this, and we have always encouraged and supported those around us. Our commitment to women's networking and mentoring has changed our lives. There are more female CEOs and business owners than ever before. More than

GRITS GLOSSARY

mentor \ 'men-,tòr\ *n* : *a person who will give you a hand to hold rather than a shove in the back; rare (except among Grits, that is; we always lend a helping hand, right, ladies?)*

25 percent of people now studying to be doctors are women. And, honey, this is just the beginning.

Grits girls are lucky enough to have a long line of women to look up to. All of us can think of a woman who served as a role model and mentor at various times in our lives: a grandmother, mother, aunt, cousin, or mother-in-law who set an example for us when we needed it most. Perhaps it was our Sunday school teacher or our Girl Scout leader who appeared at a crucial moment to offer us the tools we needed to make it through the toughest times.

The original measure of a Southern woman's success was the way she kept her home. She herself was beautiful, witty, cultured, and knew how to entertain. And if she didn't have a maid, which most women didn't, she was one hell of a cook. Over the years, being resourceful and ambitious—you can't

Third Time's a Southern Charm

BY TONE CASEY, VIRGINIA GRITS

For the most part, having a Southern accent in California has been a major asset. It seduces men and disarms your opponents. But when you're dealing with ignorant people, it can also be a negative. One time, in an Interpersonal Dynamics course at Stanford Business School, a guy with whom I had never spoken told the group that he disliked me because of my accent—he assumed that I was, in his words, a "Southern bitch." Oh well! You can't do anything about prejudice, and besides, it hasn't stopped me from becoming the three-term mayor of Los Altos Hills, California! My secret to success? I start every council meeting with a welcome and a smile for every resident in attendance, even the rude ones. That's my Southern heritage.

overestimate the ambition of a Southern woman—Grits turned those virtues into success in the world outside the home.

Southern women have always been exceptional cooks, and we've published more cookbooks than you can shake a stick at. Of course, in the South we don't take much to shaking sticks. We prefer to eat all that delicious food—and to spend all the money those books bring to the pockets of smart Southern women.

"If we ever decide to compare knees, you're going to find that I have more scars than anyone else in the room. That's because I've fallen down and gotten up so many times in my life."

—Mary Kay Ashe, Texas Grits and Founder of Mary Kay Cosmetics

Maybe this is why Lifetime Television Network named this Grits their Businesswoman of the Century!

Domesticity is only one traditional Grits virtue. Beauty is another. What beauty pageants would exist without the hard work and determination of Southern women? We didn't invent them—they go all the way back to the Trojan War—but we sure perfected them. While some folks think these contests are demeaning and outdated (Yankees all, we imagine), we Grits realize they're an important way for young women to get into college, travel, network, and turn their dreams into reality.

It's not all bathing suits and perky boobs, honey. Where would a Southern woman be without poise? And it's all for a good cause—ourselves! The Miss America Organization is the world's leading provider of scholarships for young women,

GRITS PEARL OF WISDOM #37:

The cream always rises to the top, so quit being the milkmaid. There's more to life than calluses, darlin'!

providing over $40 million in tuition assistance each year. Is it any wonder that in the last decade six Miss America winners have been Grits?

Madame Walker

Madame CJ Walker was born Sarah Breedlove on a Louisiana plantation in 1867. In 1905, she began going door-to-door selling her special hair-straightening techniques to black women. By the time she died in 1919, she was a millionaire (the rough equivalent of being a billionaire today) and not only one of the richest women, but one of the richest African-Americans in the country. Now, that's using your head—and your hair!

Recent Grits Who Became Miss America:

1993
Leanza Cornett
Jacksonville, Florida

1994
Kimberly Aiken
Columbia, South Carolina

1995
Heather Whitestone
Birmingham, Alabama

1996
Shawntel Smith
Muldrow, Oklahoma

1999
Nicole Johnson
Virginia Beach, Virginia

2000
Heather French
Maysville, Kentucky

Beauty and talent have always been bankable qualities for the Southern woman, even before Tallulah Bankhead took her dance act to Paris's Left Bank in the 1920s. Present-day stars like Kim Basinger, Tori Amos, Julia Roberts, Brandy, Cybill Shepherd, Sandra Bullock, Courteney Cox Arquette, Faith Hill, and Reese Witherspoon illustrate the breadth of success Grits have had in modeling, movies, theater, and music. Ask any man you meet: there is just something about a Southern girl. If she's a Southern girl with attitude and talent, well, it's just not a fair fight.

Our style and charm have also helped us climb to the top of the media world. Katie Couric (Virginia Grits) is just one of

the dozens of successful Southerners who have helped shape the way Americans see the world around them. A former deputy Pentagon correspondent and now coanchor of *Today*, Ms. Couric is the perfect mix of intelligent, hard-hitting reporting and honest, down-home charm. As her husband battled colon cancer, she exemplified courage and strength. After his death, Ms. Couric made fighting the disease a focus of her work and personal life. Her quest is to end the threat of colon cancer through education and research.

Grits have also taken their poise and talent for entertaining to another house: the state house. From Lillian Carter to Laura Bush, Southern women shine in the spotlight of the national stage. They don't call them first ladies for nothing! With her campaign for literacy, Laura Bush shows that a Southern girl

Pageant Time

BY KATHY STULL,
SOUTH CAROLINA GRITS

In 1976, I was one of a pack of skinny girls competing for the coveted title of "Miss Rock Hill" (South Carolina for you out-of-state people). All went well in the evening gown competition, in which I wore a then lovely, now horrible Lilli Rubin gown in a most unattractive shade of "apricot," quite possibly the worst color choice for one as fair as I. The talent competition was uneventful, as I played a lovely classical selection on the flute (yawn). My performance in the swimsuit competition, however, was a different story. It took a lot of leg makeup to make it look like blood was even running through my veins, and a good bit of pink hair tape stretched tautly across the bosoms to create the minimum amount of cleavage you would expect to see in a "scholarship" pageant, but, hey, I thought I looked pretty good at the time. Now, if I (or any other caring soul, for that matter) had been just a little bit more observant, I (or they) would have noticed a good 4 inches of string dangling out of my royal blue form-fitting swimwear ensemble and hanging jauntily between my legs. So, girls, tell your daughters to remember to check their tampon strings before sashaying around a stage in a bathing suit. By the way, I did not win, although I was a proud top five finalist. It was hard to be disappointed when the winner, my girlfriend Lavinia Cox, was crowned Miss Rock Hill. Lavinia went on to be crowned Miss South Carolina, and then first runner-up to Miss America!

knows how to use her influential position for the good of people everywhere. Just keep smiling, darlin', and keep working to make the world a better place.

A worthy cause is the best medicine in life, and it doesn't taste half-bad going down.

Politics has always been an area where Southern women excel. Texas's Barbara Jordan (1936—1996) is the perfect example of a Southern woman: fiery, moral, and inspirational. It has been said that she could dominate a room just by entering it. Barbara Jordan was and is a constant reminder that America must strive to be as good as it promises.

Taking up the current political mantle is National Secu-

Grits Political Firsts:

Hathie Wayatt Caraway (Arkansas Grits)
First woman elected to the U.S. Senate

Janet Reno (Florida Grits)
First woman Attorney General of the U.S.

Joycelyn Elders (Arkansas Grits)
First African-American to serve as Surgeon General

Keys to Persuasion, Grits Style

We've come a long way, baby, and as we've climbed to the top we've learned a few things. So here are some time-tested marketing secrets, from your sisters in the South.

- Know your customers better than you know your own dog.
- Treat your customers better than you treat your own dog.
- Dare to be different. *Classy* and different, of course.
- Tell stories about your products. If you don't have any good ones yet, go ahead and make a few up.
- Be consistent and persistent.
- Be consistent and persistent.
- Be persistent!

rity head Condoleezza Rice, an Alabama Grits who made a leap from George W. Bush's Texas staff to provost at Stanford University before returning to work as a top advisor in Mr. Bush's presidential administration. Grace, beauty, brains, confidence, and a legendary commitment to hard work and integrity: Condi Rice exemplifies successful Grits. Our country is well served by this Southern woman.

Grits have come a long way in the last three decades in another traditionally male field: business. Southern women make great leaders because we know how to be true friends. We make ourselves available to help our coworkers achieve their goals. And we know how to treat our customers. Why? Because we're better listeners than men. This is a message men in the South have traditionally ignored (do we need to tell you

A Homegrown
Success Story

*T*his is the story of a typical Southern girl. She grew up on a typical small farm in Northern, Alabama, where money was tight and Mama was a strict disciplinarian. She went to the local college and eventually ended up a high school volleyball teacher. One day, while sitting around at a hen party with her sisters in the South, she came up with an inspirational slogan and decided to make it into T-shirts for her volleyball team, which had a big game coming up the following week. The T-shirts were such a big success that people started requesting them for themselves, and even offering money for them! Soon, the woman was selling hundreds of T-shirts out of her garage every week. Next thing you know, the shirts were picked up by a major retail chain, and soon that woman had her own business, with a real staff of employees and two warehouses full of merchandise.

That person was me, of course, and the slogan I came up with that afternoon was "Grits: Girls Raised in the South." That was 1995, and now it's the twenty-first century and you're reading my book! Isn't it funny how things work out? It just goes to show that anyone can succeed if they put their mind to it. Just believe in yourself: that's the only secret to success.

—Deborah Ford

that *they never listen*?) Grits everywhere are beginning to hear it loud and clear.

Southern women have always been great storytellers. Zora Neale Hurston was one of our first great writers, but despite her later fame she died penniless. Most of her novels weren't even

WELL, I DECLARE!:
Did you know condensed milk was invented in the South? Mississipian Gail Borden introduced the concoction in 1856, and soon thereafter it became an indispensable food source for soldiers during the Civil War and beyond.

published until after her death. Since then, Grits have learned to take the money *with* the fame. It's what we deserve, after all, for bringing beauty and truth to the world.

Southern girls know their women of great letters . . .

Margaret Mitchell
Eudora Welty
Alice Walker
And how could we forget South Carolina's own Vanna White?

Three Grits Who Put the <u>First</u> in "First Lady"

Sandy Wise, first lady of West Virginia, is a successful attorney who has worked closely with the House of Representatives and former President Jimmy Carter on social security and women's issues. She currently serves on the Task Force on Child Care of the Southern Institute of Families and Children.

Rachel Gardner Hodges, first lady of South Carolina, is a former director of marketing and community relations for a hospital and an active supporter of the arts and education. She launched the statewide "Reading with Rachel" literacy program, which we think is about the coolest thing goin'.

Mary Easley, first lady of North Carolina, graduated magna cum laude from Wake Forest University and received her juris doctorate from Wake Forest School of Law. She was assistant district attorney in Hanover and Pender counties, prosecuting more than three hundred cases. Even as first lady, she continues to be a full-time professor at North Carolina Central University School of Law, where she teaches Appellate Advocacy and Criminal Trial Practice.

Margaret Mitchell's *Gone With the Wind* is now, and always will be, the classic novel of the South. Mitchell wrote it when she was recovering from an injury to her foot, and it has gone on to be one of the best-selling books of all time (it's not ever going to catch the Bible, though). Margaret Mitchell received the Pulitzer Prize for the book in May 1937, and the classic movie that followed cemented her place in our history forever.

GRITS GLOSSARY

success \ sək-'ses \ *n : something a Grits has to define for herself, simply put*

Since then, we've had a long tradition of successful novelists and writers: Eudora Welty, Flannery O'Connor, Harper Lee, and on up to present-day writers like Terry McMillan, Rebecca Wells, and Fannie Flagg.

Family Bread

It was always my dream to do a cookbook featuring all the stories and recipes from five generations of my family's women. I'd like to share one of those recipes with you. This is my grandmother's recipe for rolls. She showed me every step of this recipe, and it was one of the most special moments I have ever shared with anyone. Bread binds the family together, she always said. It's true: the bread of life is the gift of love we give to others.

—Sister Schubert, author of
Sister Schubert's Secret Bread Recipes

Sister Schubert's Special Rolls

4½ cups flour
5 teaspoons baking powder
¼ cup sugar
1 teaspoon salt
2 cups buttermilk
1 cup butter or margarine
2 packages yeast

Blend the first four ingredients together. Warm buttermilk and melt butter or margarine. Add margarine and buttermilk to dry mixture. Then add yeast—dissolved in ½ cup of lukewarm water. Mix well, until all dry ingredients are moistened and until dough is blended. Place roll batter on lightly floured surface, kneading several times. Shape into large mounds and let *rest* for 10 minutes. Roll dough out and cut with biscuit cutter. Dip each biscuit in very warm melted butter or margarine and place on baking sheet. Allow to rise and double in size (this can be 30 minutes to 1 hour). Bake at 450° for 20 minutes, or until outside is golden brown.

Following Her Father's Dream:

REVEREND BERNICE A. KING, GEORGIA GRITS

In the South, it's an honor to keep one's heritage alive, especially when that heritage is one of the most vital legacies of the region.

Reverend Bernice A. King's father was killed when she was only five years old. His death left her with a great emptiness and sense of abandonment, a wound that wasn't healed until, at seventeen, she felt the call to the ministry. Today Ms. King is assistant pastor at an inner-city church in Atlanta. In addition to her clergy work, she is a sought-after public speaker. Her focus is on leadership training and development. She has made it her priority to be a mentor for other women, from college students all the way down to elementary school girls.

Reverend King is as passionate an orator as her father, Dr. Martin Luther King, Jr., and shares his vision of racial equality and social change. "As I forge forth in my own ministry," she says, "I am beginning to understand the fact that [my father] had to sacrifice a great deal in order to fulfill his destiny and be true to what God had called him to do. He left because he had great work to do for all of us."

Writers like Maya Angelou, Alice Walker, and Toni Morrison (who's technically from Ohio but has a whole lot of Grits in her) have kept the tradition of protest literature alive. They have written passionately about the black experience in the segregated South, and have won the world over with the hard truth and lyrical beauty of their works. All three women have won major literary prizes, including Toni Morrison's Nobel Prize for Literature in 1993, the highest award given for literature each year.

> *"Though I'm grateful for the blessings of wealth, it hasn't changed who I am. My feet are still on the ground. I'm just wearing better shoes."*
>
> —Oprah Winfrey, *Mississippi Grits*

A Southern Hall of Fame would be incomplete, though, without the Southern woman to end all Southern women: Kosciusko, Mississippi's own Oprah Winfrey. Oprah's talents cut across all lines, from entertainment to acting to business to her own piece of legislation, the "Oprah Bill," a law designed to protect children from abuse. She even won a beauty contest as a teenager!

We all know Oprah, she's been in our houses more often than our husbands in many cases, and we think it's her Southern pride that helps her to stay above the trend toward trash talk in daytime television. That's why she's in the TV Hall of Fame, and has won seven Daytime Emmy Awards and the Horatio Alger Award honoring distinguished Americans who have succeeded in the face of adversity. Oprah's goal is nothing less than to change the world for the better: we think that's something all Grits should aspire to.

Pride is a precious word in our vocabulary. It is the basis of our lives as true-blue Grits. The women mentioned in this chapter are only a few of the numerous Southern women who have made us proud. Some have gained recognition through the media's efforts; others have stayed in the background and quietly made their contributions. But all have one thing in common: they've made our world a better place.

We salute our famous, infamous, and soon-to-be-famous friends in the club called Grits. We salute women who make us proud every day: those who raised families on their own, volunteer workers, country club ladies, and Junior League members who spend their time and money helping others in need. We're proud of all the mothers, grandmothers, sisters, and aunts who keep the house cool and the dinner hot. We thank the nurses, teachers, caregivers, factory workers, and checkout ladies who work every day regardless of the pay. You all make a difference in so many lives with your precious gifts.

Hope needs a foundation, and that foundation is you! Bless your hearts, every last one of you!

Grits realize that it is our unique attributes—
style, class, kindness, a little manipulation,
and a dash of harmless deceit—that help
us get ahead in business and in life.

Conclusion:

Friends Are
Forevah

*Southern Girls know . . . men may
come and go, but friends are forevah!*

$\mathcal{F}$RIENDS MATTER. THEY ARE THE BUTTER that makes our Grits so savory—and the pepper that gives them kick. They are the heirloom china that makes our parties so much fun. They are sweeter than a Southern accent and more refreshing than iced tea on a sunny verandah. They are the jokes that make us laugh until we cry, and the music that stirs our hearts. In the South, God and football aren't the only religions. Friends are part of our holy trinity, too. Often, they are the difference between living and just getting by. And, honey, in the South, we all know we want to really *live*.

GRITS PEARL OF WISDOM #39:

It's been said that love makes the world go round. That may be true, but friendship keeps the world on its axis!

True lifelong friends are more than just friends. They are a part of who we are, how we feel, how we react to situations, and how we view life's little surprises. They transcend cultures,

Sisters share a special bond...

Blood sisters
Half sisters
Stepsisters
Sorority sisters
Sisters-in-law
Soul sisters
Sisters of the South

backgrounds, and even geography. They are there in good times and in bad; they comfort and celebrate; they mature and mourn with us in our own time. The greatest gift in life is to know the true value of a friend, and to choose your friends with care.

Deep and meaningful friendships are one of the perks of being a woman. Men, bless their souls, simply don't have our capacity for connection. They think bowling, beer, and sports are enough to last a lifetime. We know a real connection doesn't come from the stomach or the television: it comes from the heart.

We've said it many times, but we'll say it here one more time: we are all sisters in the South. No matter where you come from—and even if you've never been to the South—we are all Grits if we understand that style, grace, poise, manners, and kindness are the ingredients of life, and that friendship is the butter that holds the recipe together.

There have always been, and always will be, rivalries among females. In that respect Southern girls are the same as those from other parts of the country. We are family, and like a typical family we can harbor resentment, hold a grudge, and talk each other down—behind our backs and with a smile, of course. But for Grits, friends really are forevah. No matter what our sister does or says, we know in our hearts that, in a crisis, she'll come running.

Don't ever let a friend go wanting. Don't ever be too proud to patch a rough spot. Don't ever be too stubborn to ask for help or admit your mistakes.

Friendships are worth working on, so pack that girl a basket of delicacies and drop it off at her house, even if it's not an important occasion. Throw together herbal tea, a tea set, some sandwiches and sweets, and a tablecloth, napkins, and flowers for an impromptu "tea party." Give your time to help her clean the house, organize a closet, or get some hard feelings off her chest. Friends allow us to express ourselves, so be unpredictable and defy the rules—we are here to help each other through good times and bad.

We'd love to sit down and have a tea party with each one of you, and maybe someday we will! But for now, this book is our gift to you. It contains everything sweet and spicy that these two Southern girls have learned in a lifetime. We hope you like it, and if you don't, well, we'd just as soon prefer not to hear about it, honey.

You can't choose your family, but you always choose your friends. Make this choice wisely.

Watch It, Shug

BY DIANNA BROWN MURPHREE, GRITS
AND GRANNY SMITH APPLE
GRANDMOTHER OF THE YEAR 2002

"I do declare!"
She's sugar and spice
"Well I'll swanee!"
She's everything nice.

But if you trifle with one of her sisters,
She'll tear you up like new ground, Mister.

"Bless your heart!"
She's full of grace.
"Honey, hush!"
That gorgeous face

Will spout a few well-chosen words,
And put you, Suh, right in your place.

So you best leave before you start,
'Cause Southern women love from the heart.
They cling together through thick and thin,
And nevah forsake a forevah friend.

"Y'all come back now, y'heah!"